I0066722

Praise for *People Glue*

Helen Beedham has produced a vital read for the evidence-led leader. *People Glue* is chock full of the best data and research to inform and inspire your workplace culture.

Bruce Daisley,
Author of *The Joy of Work*

Helen has written the strategic playbook for what I've been advocating for years: that trust, flexibility, and outcomes-based management aren't just nice-to-haves – they're business imperatives. Her 'four freedoms' framework gives leaders a comprehensive way to think about retention beyond just flexible work policies. Helen provides the 'why' with compelling research and a roadmap for building what she calls People Glue. If you're serious about holding onto your best talent in a rapidly evolving work world, this book belongs on your shelf right next to your strategic plans.

Brian Elliott,
CEO, Work Forward and co-author of *How the Future Works*

People Glue is a critical read for business and HR leaders who want to build organizations where people truly stick – by choice, not by force. Helen offers sharp insights, valuable frameworks, and practical strategies for leaders and individuals alike to help them create workplaces rooted in freedom and clarity of purpose. If you care about performance, retention, and making work actually work for people, *People Glue* delivers.

Siri Chilazi,
Co-author of *Make Work Fair* and
Senior Researcher at Harvard Kennedy School

In this book Helen offers an original and powerful take on retention, at a time when attracting and retaining the best talent is a crucial driver of adaptation and resilience. To want to stay, people need to experience freedom and autonomy, and Helen offers a practical framework for shaping a work culture that combines both freedom and purpose. *People Glue* is a must-read for managers and organizations who want an innovative, adaptable workforce in an era of fast-paced change.

Thomas Roulet,
Professor of Organisational Sociology and
Leadership at the Judge Business School, University of
Cambridge and co-author of *Wellbeing Intelligence*

People Glue is an essential primer for any executive who thinks seriously about what it means to lead and retain a team. It offers a clear and accessible perspective on building a great company by setting your workforce free. *People Glue* is especially valuable for managers grappling with the human side of leadership for the first time.

Robert Pickering,
Chair, Marex Group plc, author of *Blue Blood:*
Cazenove in the age of global banking

People Glue is an essential read for any business leader focused on retaining talent as a competitive edge. In this brilliantly practical book, Helen reveals the real reasons why people leave and what makes the difference in organizations who get it right. Drawing on a rich analysis, Helen uncovers the often-surprising elements that bind people, teams, and cultures, offering tools and techniques to apply these insights in our own organizations.

Sinéad Keenan,
Chief Innovation Officer, EZRA Coaching

People Glue is essential reading for leaders and employees who want to be part of high-performing organizations, able to navigate the steep obstacles of business life today. Helen backs up her claim that setting people free is likely to make them stay by explaining compellingly the consequences and benefits of this freedom. With thorough and thoughtful analysis, she shows why it can be so hard to create freedom in organizations; the dangers of false freedoms, and the pitfalls that can arise on this journey, but also provides a clear roadmap on how to deliver freedom and thus create the employee commitment craved by many leaders. By the end, I was clear about the prize, positive about the journey, and keen to make a start.

Jonathan Bond,
HR Director, Leigh Day and author of *Workolution*

This book is laser-focused on why people matter. I love how Helen explains the principle of purpose, both for the business and also for the individual, so it aligns for maximum performance – why you should give a damn! Belonging as a concept for the best talent retention and most importantly the power of freedom and autonomy driven through an organization to really make People Glue effective. A brilliant read for anyone wanting to grow a business with people at the core.

Sam Smith,
Co-Founder of The Superscalers,
former CEO of finnCap and author of *The Secret Sauce*

Helen has expertly sculpted a practical guidebook to ensure that business purpose can be realized through a motivated 'sticky' team. It tackles some of the moment's toughest debates such as pay and flexibility, to give advice on how they can be harnessed sustainably to motivate talented people to stay, and to perform. Powerful for HR leaders and individuals alike, I'd recommend *People Glue* to anyone who believes that people, purpose, and performance are the key to changing the world.

Ruth Handcock OBE,
CEO, Octopus Money

People Glue

Hold on to your best people by setting them free

HELEN BEEDHAM

First published in Great Britain by Practical Inspiration Publishing, 2026

© Helen Beedham, 2026

The moral rights of the author have been asserted.

ISBN   9781788607773 (hardback)
         9781788607780 (paperback)
         9781788607797 (epub)

All rights reserved. This book, or any portion thereof, may not be reproduced without the express written permission of the publisher.

Every effort has been made to trace copyright holders and to obtain their permission for the use of copyright material. The publisher apologizes for any errors or omissions and would be grateful if notified of any corrections that should be incorporated in future reprints or editions of this book.

EU GPSR representative: LOGOS EUROPE, 9 rue Nicolas Poussin, LA ROCHELLE 17000, France Contact@logoseurope.eu

Want to bulk-buy copies of this book for your team and colleagues? We can customize the content and co-brand *People Glue* to suit your business's needs.

Please email info@practicalinspiration.com for more details.

Practical Inspiration
Publishing

For Judith

and in memory of Nicholas.

Contents

Foreword

The power of People Glue

WHAT IF YOUR organization could become magnetic –
drawing in top talent, inspiring loyalty, and unlocking the
full potential of every individual? In a world where complexity,
change, and competition are constants, the ability to create
a culture that sticks is no longer a luxury – it's a leadership
imperative. That's where People Glue comes in.

This book is not just timely – it's transformative. It offers a fresh,
research-backed framework for building organizations where
people thrive, take ownership, and drive performance from within.
At its heart, People Glue is about creating the conditions for trust,
psychological safety, and meaningful engagement – conditions
that allow people to do their best work and leaders to lead with
clarity and purpose.

When I first met Helen, I was immediately struck by her deep
empathy for the challenges leaders face today. Her insights are
grounded in rigorous research, rich conversations with CEOs and
senior leaders, and her own lived experience. She understands the
pressures that come from every direction – internal demands,
external volatility, and the relentless pace of change. What makes

this book so powerful is how she translates that understanding into actionable wisdom.

Helen introduces a compelling new concept: People Glue. It's more than a metaphor – it's a mindset and a method. Through this lens, leaders are invited to reimagine their role, not as controllers of outcomes, but as architects of environments where people are free to grow, make decisions, express themselves, and find meaning in their work.

The book is structured in four parts, each building on the last to create a comprehensive roadmap for cultural transformation and leadership enhancement finding meaning in their work.

What sets this book apart is its dual focus: it speaks to the needs of employees and the aspirations of leaders. It challenges us to think differently, to lead more humanely, and to build cultures that are not only high-performing but deeply fulfilling.

As a CEO, this book has prompted me to ask better questions, to listen more deeply, and to lead with greater intention. It has reminded me that leadership is not about having all the answers – it's about creating the space for others to shine.

In a time when many leaders feel overwhelmed and under-resourced, *People Glue* offers both a compass and a call to action. It is a powerful reminder that when we invest in people, we invest in performance, and when we create cultures that stick, we build organizations that last.

Dr Arlene Egan
CEO, Roffey Park Institute

Introduction

'In the middle of difficulty lies opportunity.'

Albert Einstein

Who'd want to lead a business today?

L ET'S BE HONEST, growing a successful, enduring business amidst a dizzying kaleidoscope of challenges, both external and internal to the organization, calls for superhuman abilities that would bring out any superhero's imposter syndrome.

Casting a glance externally first, geopolitical uncertainty and conflicts reshape the energy markets, trade flows and the supply chains that underpin the daily operations of businesses around the world. In parallel, protectionist economic policies, new strategic defence alliances and shifting coalitions continually refashion the international order while global superpowers compete to extend their influence and access to valuable natural resources in other regions. Big tech firms disrupt and reshape entire industries and raise the bar in terms of consumers' expectations of speed and personalization, forcing other businesses to swiftly adapt or die. The COVID-19 pandemic that reverberated throughout the business world compelled leaders everywhere to transform their traditional modus operandi in the space of a few weeks and months and brought employee wellbeing out from the shadows, into the spotlight and onto the top of executive agendas everywhere. These kinds of events and developments have a major impact on inflation: in recent years they've brought an end to a period of relatively low, stable inflation and prompted higher inflation. At the time of writing, gloomy global growth forecasts anticipate a looming economic recession. Given all the above, small wonder that 90% of CEOs are concerned about macroeconomic conditions[1] as they try to steer their organizations forward.

Turning our gaze now inside the organization, the apparent post-pandemic return of 'business as usual' masked a more accurate case of 'same, same but different' as worker expectations and employment practices and norms continuously evolve. Alongside the need to acknowledge and support employee wellbeing there have been parallel trends adding to CEOs' considerations, some comfortingly linear and predictable but others more zigzag and erratic in nature. The viral spread of the #MeToo movement in October 2017 sparked discussions in workplaces about sexual discrimination and harassment, leading in the UK to the amendment of the Equality Act with a new onus on employers to take 'reasonable steps' to prevent such harassment. The murder of George Floyd in America in May 2020 saw organizations everywhere sprint to invest more resources, both people and financial, in their diversity, equity and inclusion (DEI) efforts before the second Trump administration's swift dismantling of DEI resources and policies caused those same organizations to reconsider their public stance and adopt a more nuanced, under-the-radar approach.

The rise of digital work tools, technology and global mobility, the seductive lure of entrepreneurship and portfolio careers, and the demise of the 'job for life' that characterized previous generations' careers have all contributed to the ongoing war for talent. Indeed, the competition for sought-after skills and expertise is hotter than ever and at the same time, employees are more aware of the alternative possibilities that ping loudly and frequently on their career radars and are more motivated to explore these.

So today's leader has to figure out, with their board and executive team, a profitable path forward in a fast-changing context with employees who are looking to them for a meaningful career on customized terms and a robust moral compass. In the words of one chief executive I spoke to, 'I don't think there's ever been as much thrown at a CEO as there is right now'.

The quest for glue

Speaking with those who have the drive, skills, and steeliness to take on this challenge, I hear leaders ponder how to:

- Balance employees' needs and aspirations with the commercial and operational realities of the business.
- Acknowledge individual preferences in a workforce that is generationally, racially, and socially diverse.
- Continue offering hybrid- and remote-working without employees becoming more emotionally and physically disconnected from work.
- Reduce their higher-than-desired level of employee turnover without sending the pay bill through the roof.
- Minimize the loss of valued individuals in business-critical roles who have grown up 'through the ranks' and accumulated hard-to-replace expertise.
- Prevent people they've significantly invested in – such as graduates, returners, people from diverse backgrounds, and far-flung talent with in-demand skills and expertise – from walking out the door after a relatively short time.

These concerns are mirrored in the rates of employee turnover that have been steadily increasing globally over the past five years,[2] hovering at around 35% in the UK and 46% in the US.

If these are some of the challenges, then what does success look like if you're leading a business?

Of course, your ambition is, in part, to ensure a satisfying financial return to the managing partners, private equity firms, or public shareholders who have staked often sizeable investments in your organization. This involves growing the income streams and managing down costs including employee turnover costs.

But there is a deeper, richer outcome that you're setting your sights on.

While wanting to grow the bottom line and keep stakeholders happy, success also means uniting everyone in the organization, harnessing the potential achievements and discretionary effort that each individual can contribute, and inspiring your employees to stay for the longer term.

You're doing this by cultivating a set of beliefs and behaviours that everyone buys into and is motivated by; that holds the team firm when the winds of change and uncertainty buffet the business; that sets you apart from competitors and acts as a beacon drawing desirable clients and customers in through the door; and that brings the promised 'deal' agreed between employer and employee to life in a mutually rewarding way day in, day out.

You're striving to build a winning culture that binds people – employees, partners, suppliers, and clients, but especially your employees – together. You acknowledge that for your business to continue to exist a decade from now, let alone flourish, you need a flexible, skilled, and loyal workforce that commits to staying for the longer-term. You are clear that retaining your valued workers is the most important source of competitive advantage – a vital springboard that will launch your business forward – and you are prepared to leave behind long-entrenched management credos, structures, and mindsets in order to achieve this.

You are looking to create People Glue.

Bedrock beliefs

Each industry has its own dynamics and characteristics; each business sets out their specific goals; each CEO brings their own vision and leadership style. But across this multiplicity of variations, leaders who want to create a winning culture adhere, to a greater or lesser extent, to a common set of bedrock beliefs that underpin everything they do. These can be summarized as:

1. *An employee is more than a number.* While people today might not expect to stay with one employer for a decade or more, equally they don't want to be treated as a depersonalized, instantly replaceable resource – or worse, not replaced at all. People's experience of work and at work matters, even in the largest organizations where the risk of feeling like a small, anonymous cog in an enormous machine is highest.
2. *Workplaces should be human-centred.* Employees are people first, workers second; we are complex beings with physical, mental, emotional, developmental, social, and spiritual needs that cannot be locked away and ignored during our hours of work. By recognizing and supporting people's needs, you can tap more fully into their abilities and potential and create strong communities.
3. *Openness matters.* While some business information is inevitably market-sensitive and/or subject to legal protections, today's forward-thinking executives believe in sharing as much information as openly as possible within the organization, and with partners and suppliers too, and trusting their people to make decisions and figure out the best way to meet clients' needs.
4. *Focus on the sweet spot.* For many employees, their job is just one element of their life* and other elements vie for their time, energy, and attention including their home lives, health, alternative work options including self-employment

---

* I want to recognize that for someone in insecure circumstances, their job may provide a vital lifeline that takes priority above everything else.

and competitor organizations, future plans and dreams, and retirement. Likewise, a business must clearly set out the path it is on and can't afford to bend endlessly to the wills and desires of all who work there. But by focusing on the sweet spot where both parties' interests and ambitions align, your business will benefit.

My story

When I look back over my 30-year career to date and reflect on my different experiences of work, one chapter sticks in my memory because for me, and I think for my employer too, it hit the 'sweet spot':

- *I had some serious fun at work.* Spontaneous, laughter-filled lunches and evenings out with my colleagues; awaydays and corporate celebrations at the company's expense where we could (and did!) let our hair down; occasional tickets to high-profile events and posh client 'do's'. I even met my wonderful husband there.
- *I smashed a few self-limiting beliefs.* Roles, projects, and clients stretched me far outside of my comfort zone with mentors at my elbow; these tough experiences taught me I was capable of more than I'd previously thought and silenced my imposter syndrome for a welcome spell or two.
- *I had adventures.* I travelled to places in the UK and around the world that I'd probably never have visited otherwise, from Chester to Cape Town, Southampton to San Francisco, Keswick to Kuala Lumpur, and I got to spend time with people with fascinatingly different lives to mine.
- *I figured out (gradually) who I was.* I was encouraged to experiment with my personality and explore my strengths; I grew in self-awareness and confidence and built my professional brand.

- *I was treated like an adult.* Back in the late nineties and the noughties, where I worked we were all trusted to get on and deliver without having to account for every moment or be visible. We were judged on what we delivered and what we'd been like to work with, and that was pretty much it.
- *I was cared for.* When the chips were down and life was throwing its worst at me – the sudden death of my father at 59, a long-term relationship break-up, unexplained infertility – my manager and my colleagues supported me in so many ways and helped me through.

When opportunities elsewhere came close to enticing me away, it was all these reasons that persuaded me to stay, for 15 years.

Navigating this book

If you've picked up this book, you're probably curious to discover how to offer more freedom to the brilliant people who work in your business so they'll do their best work for you and stay for longer.

Perhaps you're frustrated that nothing you've tried to date has improved employee retention and engagement in an already tight labour market? Are you wanting to differentiate your business more clearly in a crowded industry? Or maybe your business is going through a major transition and you want employees to embrace new mindsets and ways of working to fuel your growth?

If so, *People Glue* is for you. It will help you formulate the 'deal' you can offer to attract and retain a diverse workforce with the skills and expertise that your business needs. In parallel, it will help you determine whether people's *experience* of work in your organization is living up to that promise, and what to do if it isn't. *People Glue* draws on my own expertise in organization- and team-effectiveness honed over the last 30 years and extensive primary and secondary research I have conducted including conversations with numerous business and people leaders listed in the Acknowledgements.

My advice won't hit the mark for everyone. If your business doesn't care about fostering a shared sense of beliefs and/or you don't believe more freedom will work for your business, then that's fine – as long as you're transparent about this. As my teenager says, 'keep it real'. If you're still with me, then let me guide you briefly through the pages that follow.

In Part 1, I'll look at what makes organizations 'sticky'. Find out what People Glue is and how to assess how 'sticky' your organization is today; why people typically choose to stay or leave their employer and why *your* people are leaving *you*.

Part 2 explores the concept of freedom at work, by first unpacking what freedom at work today is and isn't, then taking you on a pacy sprint through the evolution of freedom at work. It introduces you briefly to the four freedoms and the numerous 'anti-freedom' forces that could derail your ambitions.

Part 3 puts each of the four freedoms under the microscope and offers examples of what other organizations are doing that benefits employees and the business, to inspire your own plans.

Part 4 provides a practical blueprint for how you can operationalize freedom in your organization and how best to respond if and when freedom falters. Discover what offering greater freedom means for you personally as a leader and how to successfully turn managers into freedom coaches who encourage and empower their teams.

In the Conclusion I offer three hopes for how you might put the insights in this book to use and a heartfelt appeal for why People Glue matters for business, society and the generations that follow us.

Let's get going.

Part 1
'Sticky'
organizations

'To keep a lamp burning, we have to keep putting oil in it.'
Mother Teresa

Chapter 1
People Glue

'Coming together is a beginning, staying together is progress, and working together is success.'

Attributed to Henry Ford

Let's start with the big question: what exactly is People Glue?

IF YOU'RE THINKING that People Glue sounds uncomfortably intangible and hard to pin down, that's understandable. At this point, People Glue might indeed resemble a dark art: a difficult-to-grasp concept, shrouded in mystique, that is rooted deep in the human psyche and the very nature of our existence.

Granted, we're clearly not talking about easily knowable, identifiable 'stuff' that can be listed on spreadsheets and tracked in project plans. However, some consistent features of People Glue often emerge in my conversations with business leaders; these features are backed up by a wide body of external research into people's experiences of their work and the characteristics of successful organizations.

In this chapter, I'll demystify People Glue by explaining what you hear when it exists and what you see; whether every organization needs it or not and when you might need extra glue; and why People Glue isn't easy to create or apply in practice. In later chapters, I'll set out in more detail the components of People Glue and how you can build it into the way you operate in your organization.

When People Glue exists here's what you hear

'I believe in this'

Pretty much all of the leaders I've spoken with agree that the most fundamental aspect of People Glue is a clear and compelling *purpose*: your reason for existing as a business. This starts with talking about the outcomes that you're seeking to achieve for your customers; if there's any fogginess about this, you're missing a vital opportunity to unite people around a common goal. Crucially, purpose isn't a one-way street: it's not just about what your organization is there to achieve, nor is it just about the personal purpose that motivates each employee. It's about the alignment of *both* of these purposes. When the organization and individual goals are in sync, a deep motivation emerges. People give a damn.

The following findings from recent UK[1] and US[2] studies illustrate how much purpose matters to leaders and workers alike:

- 79% of executive leaders consider purpose to be central to their business' success.
- 83% of UK workers rank 'finding meaning in day-to-day work' as their top priority and most of these would change employers to secure this.
- 93% of US working adults believe it's very or somewhat important to have a job where they feel the work has meaning.
- A third of employees would sacrifice pay for a different role which was more fulfilling.

'I know my part'

We often hear the well-known phrase 'all politics is local'; in the world of work, 'all purpose is local'. In other words, your purpose has to make sense and feel meaningful to everyone across your business. As a leader you can talk about your financial and operational performance in clear factual terms (and this has its value), but unless people in different roles and different locations across your business understand how they're directly contributing to this performance, you're missing a vital trick.

People need to know what *part* they're playing in the bigger purpose and how they can fulfil that in their day-to-day work. Linking your mission – your big, hairy, audacious goals – directly to individual roles requires an organization-wide goal-setting framework such as OKRs (objectives and key results), some KPIs (key performance indicators) which track your progress, and team- and individual-level performance objectives, plus consistent messages from you and your fellow leaders about what's important and recognition of parts well played.

At the same time when there's plenty of Glue around your people will forgive a lot; people expect their employer to play their part but they'll also be pragmatic and accept their organization's imperfections. As one global people leader memorably summed it up to me, they 'can tolerate a lot of crap'.

'We're in this together'

A third aspect of People Glue is people having the sense that they are *connected* to the wider work and to one another. By wider work, I mean work done by other teams aside from their own. Often the sense of shared purpose and belonging is much higher *within* teams than *across* teams and organizations can suffer from what General Stanley McChrystal, the US Army General who led the Joint Special Operations Task Force in Iraq, terms as 'blinks' – weaknesses in horizontal connectivity that become 'choke points' hampering effective communication and performance.

In terms of interpersonal connections, these are strongest in human-centric organizations, also described as 'radically human' workplaces, where the fostering of strong social bonds and of compassion and care for one another is prioritized as highly as the efficient execution of tasks and achievement of goals. Robin Dunbar, Professor of Evolutionary Psychology at the University of Oxford and author of numerous books including *The Social Brain: the psychology of successful organizations*, told me on my podcast:

> If you're dealing with organizations, you're dealing with a community. It's a village. No matter what else it might be doing. It's a village and the efficiency with which it's going to work and do its job and even come up with clever new ideas depends on the quality of the relationships between the members of that village.

Research by Korn Ferry Consulting bears this out: radically human organizations grow faster, innovate better, and have a more highly motivated workforce with employee engagement scores of 90% and higher.[3]

So, People Glue is about purpose, part, and connection.

Here's what it's *not*

- *Generic across all organizations, everywhere.* It is unique to your business. People Glue needs to be tailored to your purpose, your context, and your values, otherwise what is there to differentiate you from any other business?
- *The same thing to everyone.* It means slightly different things to each person in your organization (more on the challenges of that later). But you can meet many different employees' sweet spots (see Introduction) with your organization's brand of People Glue.

- *A rigid, one-way street.* It's a two-way contract that evolves over time. It can be offered but not imposed on people as ultimately they'll choose whether they want to buy into it or not. They'll help shape your People Glue through their perspectives and their contributions to your business.
- *A single workplace policy.* It's about a shared value system established and reinforced over time. Businesses often misguidedly look for a silver bullet that will magically meet your workforce's needs and your organization's needs at the same time. This is a futile search because it's not down to your annual leave or your hybrid-working policy – it comes from your purpose and the way you choose to live that purpose every single day.

Does every organization need People Glue?

It may surprise you that my answer is no. Let me be clear, I'm wholeheartedly in favour of purpose-led, human-centric, compassionate organizations, and believe these result in higher performance over longer timescales compared to organizations that don't have those characteristics.

But organizations can still be successful without such characteristics. They can offer a far more transactional relationship between employer and employee on markedly different terms. This tends to be seen in places like investment banks and top-tier law firms, but it also plays out in more entrepreneurial environments particularly in the technology sector. In the former, the deal is broadly characterized by high levels of remuneration in return for extremely long hours, high-pressure workloads, and an expectation that work comes first, home lives second. In the latter, it's about 'high risk, high reward' stakes where individuals also work long working weeks (and weekends and holidays) in return for lower pay today and an equity stake that could pay off big time if and when the company IPOs (floats on the Stock Exchange). As long as leaders and hiring managers are fully transparent about the deal on offer from the outset, this approach can still meet the needs of both employer and employee.

In the same vein, not every individual is fussed about finding organizations that explicitly care for their needs, preferences, and wellbeing. Ambitious investment bankers and corporate lawyers are attracted to big-name firms for the chance to make serious amounts of money in the early-mid stages of their career which then (in theory at least) frees up their options for their later working years. They are also more likely to work on high-profile deals and develop cutting-edge services and solutions. Those working in early-stage businesses often relish the opportunity to shape something new and exciting for an untapped market while enjoying the relative lack of structure and hierarchy in a young organization.

Some professionals treat their CV like a stock whereby they view each career move as a 'trade', an investment in their career from which they hope to yield maximum reward within a relatively short timeframe. They have a higher appetite for risk and see first-hand experience of organizational failure – sometimes multiple failures – adding to their CV and marketability, not detracting. For these individuals, their career story is more attractive to prospective employers because they have had unusual or extraordinary experiences, regardless of whether these were ultimately successful or not over the longer term.

Assuming you do subscribe to the belief that a more human-centric ethos and approach generates higher levels of performance and greater value, you may be wondering how you can tell, other than through gut instinct, whether you've got People Glue in your organization. There are certain signs set out below – some easily identifiable, others less so – that can quickly give you a robust indication of this; think of them as observable cues. Towards the end of this chapter is a diagnostic that you can use with your leadership team or HR leader to assess in a more structured way how 'sticky' your organization is right now.

Glue cues

As you read through this list, make a mental note of which ones you swiftly tick as a 'yes' and which ones cause you to hesitate. What makes you so confident about the former? What evidence comes to mind? And with the hesitations, what's bothering you here? This quick exercise can give you an initial steer on where to recognize your successes and where to focus further investigations for a more definitive conclusion.

1. *People are staying.* Your headline retention rate will tell you whether you're in line with your industry average, the detail tells you what's actually going on. Look at different demographics, functional areas, and seniority levels, and how these rates have been changing over the past three to five years.

2. *People aren't being poached by competitors.* There will always be reasons why people choose to leave that aren't related to your organization and don't suggest a glue issue – a change in career, ill health, relocating for their partner's job, for example. But if competitors are picking off your employees at a steady rate, then you've got cause for concern.

3. *People are going above and beyond.* They're not just meeting expectations, they're doing their best work. In management speak this is termed 'discretionary effort' and typically measured via employee engagement scores. And it matters: in one CEO's words, 'if you're missing this, it can be the difference between success and failure'. In 'best practice' organizations 72% of employees are engaged while the global average is 23%.[4]

4. *People are thriving.* They are in good health, performing well, and growing personally and professionally. When

people are flourishing at work they are less likely to leave and almost twice as likely to stay for two or more years.

5. *People are joyful.* While it might feel a stretch expecting employees to be in raptures about their work, it does matter that they are positive and upbeat. Happy workers are less likely to say they would consider taking a new job than less happy ones and as employee satisfaction rises, the likelihood of their applying elsewhere diminishes.

6. *People are acting as ambassadors.* They speak highly of your organization to others and are up to seven times more likely to recommend your company as an employer. As a useful benchmark to compare to, at UK-based Great Place to Work Certified companies 86% of employees say they would recommend their organization to others.

Times when you need extra glue

Just as there are times in our professional or personal lives when we need to draw more deeply on our reserves, so too there are times in the lifecycle of an organization when more People Glue is called for. This might happen when you're going through a major milestone in your expansion or maturity, for example, shifting from being the nimble new player hoovering up market share to becoming an established player with a stable slice of the 'pie' and needing to figure out alternative growth strategies. Long-standing employees may feel they're losing valued access to the CEO and other senior leaders or having their freedom to operate curtailed by new committees, structures, and processes.

If you've ever experienced a major organizational restructuring as a result of a merger, acquisition, spin-off, or cost-reduction exercise, you'll have witnessed firsthand how People Glue can be at its most brittle during such periods. The often-stressful upheaval and uncertainty about the future – particularly 'what does this mean for me?' – can become a flashpoint for people to re-evaluate their jobs and the impetus to move on to something new, or at least different.

Your shared sense of purpose, the clarity of the part each person plays and your connection and cohesion as a group might also be tested in a founder-led business when the original founder and CEO either steps into a different role or retires from the organization completely. Founder CEOs are often charismatic individuals with a compelling vision, and it's common for them to have been personally involved in recruiting employees; with a new CEO's arrival, people may feel a sense of loss that calls into question their ongoing relationship with the organization.

The dark side of People Glue

We saw earlier in this chapter how tightly People Glue is linked to your purpose as a business, however, an inherent paradox lies at its heart. Your purpose acts as a magnet drawing people to you, it's why they want to join and what persuades them to stay. But CEOs tell me it has a dark side too: in mission-led organizations, people hold leaders very firmly to that mission and can quickly switch from supporters to detractors if they feel you are making decisions that don't appear to sit comfortably with your mission. So, if employees aren't in favour of a shift in business strategy, a major product-related decision, or a new workplace policy that departs from your previous approach they may object, often quite vocally, that this transgresses your stated purpose.

Another way that purpose can be a double-edged sword is this: they may join your business because they feel a strong affinity with your social purpose (so far, so good) but wrongly expect to have an easier ride because they think performance expectations will be softer (not so good). In fact, the performance bar is likely to be *higher* because in reality, it is far more difficult to achieve both commercial and social purpose outcomes because you may not have access to the same income or funding opportunities as purely commercial entities.

The perception of your employer brand in the market can create another minefield to navigate. Candidates today don't just look at how financially competitive your offer is, they also scrutinize your workplace policies, public statements, ESG (environmental, social, and governance) strategy, and DEI (diversity, equity, and inclusion) records to decide whether yours is an organization in which they want to invest their time and energy. It can be quite a challenge from a business leader's perspective not to let one or two individual policies frame your reputation in the marketplace. Equally, shrugging your collective shoulders and concluding 'well, it's just the market, it's just the way younger people think' is an inadequate response. People have become more aware of other opportunities which offer greater flexibility while paying the same or more. In response, it's important to work out what individual people need and want to inspire them to stay.

Finally, if you're an execution-focused leader who likes to draw a line under completed achievements and fling your energies into the next priorities in your pipeline, then take a deep breath. People Glue doesn't come with an end date and the notion that at some point you've set the organization up in perpetuity is a hollow one. You have to *keep* investing in your offer to employees and the experience of work that they have, because the market is constantly evolving and so too are people's expectations. As one business leader said to me 'you can never close the box on this'.

So, People Glue has inherent tensions, it can lead to problematic sticking points and cultivating it can feel uncomfortably like painting the Forth Bridge.* But these challenges pale in comparison with the benefits your business stands to gain if you get this right. So, let's take a look now at how 'sticky' your organization is today.

* The Forth Bridge is an iconic cantilever railway bridge located in Scotland, designated a UNESCO World Heritage Site. It requires a continuous cycle of maintenance and repainting and so colloquially it symbolizes any task without a definite end point.

Advice for leaders

If you lead a business, then you may have an instinctive sense of how strong your People Glue is today from certain workforce data and/or conversations with different individuals. However, it's easy to draw conclusions in haste from limited or skewed data points or from information that we're unconsciously overweighting. To process information at speed, our brains rely on mental shortcuts known as biases and heuristics, and while this is incredibly helpful (we don't want to have to read the full description of coffees available when we're ordering our morning caffeine hit) it's also laden with cognitive pitfalls. For example, we typically rely on information that is more easily obtainable (the 'availability' heuristic), that backs up what our gut feel is telling us (the 'confirmation' bias), or that shows up first in a list or in time (the 'anchoring' bias).

The Freedom Index below can help you counter these thinking traps. Take 15 minutes to work through the questions, noting both your rating for each statement *and* the evidence that is informing your answer. At the end, look at your overall pattern of responses to assess how healthy your People Glue is right now and notice where any data gaps are. You can also use this tool for a specific team or business unit if you're a team leader or a senior manager.

Freedom index

Statement	Rating						Evidence
	Strongly disagree	Disagree	Neutral	Agree	Strongly agree	Don't know	
1. We're able to attract high quality candidates.	•	•	•	•	•	•	
2. Our employees are engaged and motivated.	•	•	•	•	•	•	

(continued)

Statement	Rating						Evidence
	Strongly disagree	Disagree	Neutral	Agree	Strongly agree	Don't know	
3. People participate enthusiastically in in-person working and social events.	•	•	•	•	•	•	
4. People actively recommend us to others.	•	•	•	•	•	•	
5. People pursue other interests successfully alongside their roles here.	•	•	•	•	•	•	
6. People move around the business easily here.	•	•	•	•	•	•	
7. We can often fill senior roles from internal talent pools.	•	•	•	•	•	•	
8. Average tenure is above market levels across all age categories.	•	•	•	•	•	•	
9. Many people leave us for external reasons unrelated to the organization.	•	•	•	•	•	•	
10. We don't have problematic vacancies that remain unfilled for long periods.	•	•	•	•	•	•	
11. A good proportion of leavers 'boomerang' back to us later.	•	•	•	•	•	•	
12. Former colleagues often become our clients.	•	•	•	•	•	•	

Advice for individuals

If you don't have people management or business management responsibility, you can still benefit from reflecting on what is making you choose to stay with your current employer. And if you haven't decided whether you're staying or going then as Annie Duke, former professional poker player, cognitive psychologist, and author of *Quit*, says, by default you're choosing the status quo.

To turn that into a more intentional decision, consider the following questions:

1. How committed do I feel to this organization and why?
2. How well aligned is my personal purpose with where this organization wants to go?
3. How well do I know what is expected of me and how I can contribute?
4. How confident do I feel that I have the requisite skills and capabilities to perform well?
5. How much do I trust my immediate manager and senior leaders?
6. When did I last have fun at work?
7. Do I have a valued friend (or a few friends) at work?
8. How well does my role meet my needs and priorities at this point in my life?

Seasons or lifetimes

A few years ago, I was speaking with someone I knew in the rural community where we live. He was a vicar and he was letting me know that his long marriage to his wife was ending. After sympathizing, I was curious to know how the news of his impending divorce had been received by his seniors in the church. He shared that the bishop had been very empathetic, observing of marriages that 'some last for a season, others last for a lifetime'. That poetic description could just as well apply to our relationships with our employers too, although jobs 'for a lifetime' are less common today than a few decades ago. I'll turn now to the question of what makes us stay, what makes us leave, and what factors influence our loyalty.

Chapter 2
Why people stay

'Life must be understood backward. But it must be lived forward.'
Søren Kierkegaard

Crossing the road

IN EARLY SUMMER 1997, I'd hopped off the bus and was crossing the road towards the entrance of South Kensington tube station in west London when it dawned on me. It was time for me to leave my first employer, after two years. I stayed with my next employer for 15 years and have often reflected on what persuaded me to dedicate such a large portion of my life to that second organization.

As people, we're all gloriously different in our motivations, our needs, and our ambitions, while our home lives and financial situations vary enormously. So, what appeals to me about my job could make you shudder with aversion or sigh with relief that you're *not* in that job, organization, or industry. Yet despite this infinite plurality of views, there are some consistent threads that emerge as reasons why people choose to stay with their employer. In this chapter, I'll explore these influences and in particular the powerful interplay between three critical factors. You'll discover what inspires loyalty, what causes employees to 'cross the road' and how people are feeling about their futures at work.

Goodbye jobs for life

Up to and including my parents' generation (born during World War II), staying in the same job for life was not just accepted, it was the norm. In comparison, the average tenure today is dramatically shorter; in the US it is just under four years[1] while in the UK it is between two to four years. On this basis we can expect to work for up to 12 different organizations throughout a 50-year career.

This decline of the job for life was partly driven by the dwindling of traditional industries such as manufacturing and the rise of service-based sectors. With computer networks and the internet, work and talent globalized, and access to cheaper skilled labour in other geographies via outsourcing and offshoring took off. Job security was also threatened by the emergence of new competitors undercutting or outpacing complacent businesses. Restructuring and redundancies severed many people's belief in a job for life while online job portals, remote working, and the gig economy have motivated workers to craft a better deal for themselves.

Our desire to stay put varies by life stage and by our organization's life stage. Early in our careers we often value the accumulation of skills, experience, and adventures; with mid-life, mortgages, and/or young children we may place higher value on stability and predictability; and as older workers, passing on our expertise to younger colleagues and accessing healthcare and pension benefits make us minded to stay.

A company's appeal to employees will vary at different points in its lifecycle: some find the unstructured dynamism of start-up or scale-up businesses an irresistible magnet, others prefer the more corporate set-up of a larger, more established player. Even long-tenure employees flirt with breaking up at major transitions such as a change of ownership, a grinding transformation, or a disruptive acquisition.

Why people stay

This question has been extensively explored in organizational psychology and the answer is multi-faceted; it's also still evolving. Three helpful theories and models, presented below in chronological order, offer a good starting point for understanding what influences people's motivation and choices in life and at work:

1. Abraham Maslow's Hierarchy of Needs posits that security and the ability to meet one's essential daily needs take precedent over higher-order needs such as esteem, belonging and self-fulfilment.
2. Frederick Herzberg's Two-Factor Theory also differentiates between 'hygiene' factors like pay and security, and 'motivator' factors such as opportunities to grow, with the two groups co-existing separately rather than as a continuum.
3. Richard Ryan and Edward Deci's Self-Determination Theory explains how sources of intrinsic or internal motivation such as curiosity and purpose are more powerful drivers than extrinsic levers such as employer-led rewards or sanctions.

From my research and conversations with leaders, the following considerations (not presented in order of influence) play into people's decisions to stay in a role and with their employer:

1. *'It's the economy, stupid'.** During economic downturns, job security ascends in priority as we feel less confident about landing a job elsewhere.
2. *Stability.* For some of us, familiarity and continuity matter more than ambition and growth. The experienced, dependable employees who stay in broadly the same role for 20-plus years bring vital operational stability to their organizations.

---

* Election slogan coined by James Carville, chief strategist for Bill Clinton's 1992 presidential campaign.

3. *Excitement.* Another swathe of the workforce crave the excitement that comes from disrupting, innovating, and making an impact. Having the chance to make a difference, whether early on or in a final career push, makes us more likely to stay.[†]

4. *Appreciation.* If we receive high-quality recognition for our contribution and performance, we are less likely to leave our jobs after two years. We like to feel loved!

5. *Identity.* Our sense of identity is strongly linked to the job that we do, so changing jobs can be a deeply-rooted, pandora's-box-inducing decision. Even when we hate our current job, it takes a lot to decide to move. One CEO likened our reluctance to move jobs to our dislike of moving house – unless it's a magnificent upgrade, we put it off for as long as we can and even then we know we're not going to be very happy with the movers.

The golden triangle

Three critical considerations lie at the heart of people's decisions to keep investing in the status quo, as shown in Figure 1.

Figure 1 The golden triangle

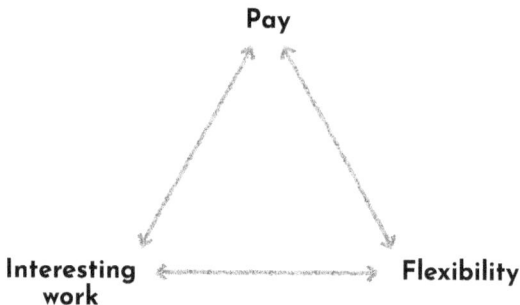

† It's easier for higher-income earners working in professional roles to leave an employer for purpose-related reasons than it is for those working in lower paid jobs with less financial security.

To paraphrase George Orwell and *Animal Farm,* all factors are equal but some factors are more equal than others. The following three are the biggies, they're interlinked and here's how they influence the stay/go decision.

1. Pay

Many assume that people jump ship for better pay. This is rarely true, for the following reasons.

First, compensation addresses people's basic needs and provides financial security, it ticks the 'survive' box but not the 'thrive' box. That's why employee turnover rises with inflation: people seek better pay elsewhere in order to cover their higher living costs.

Second, it's personal. Our mindset and decision about what's an acceptable level of pay varies depending on our life stage, our age, and our circumstances. For working parents, flexibility of working pattern may trump salary progression for a while; for those needing to rebuild their finances after a costly divorce or pay off loans after higher or executive education, negotiating the highest possible salary or bonus may feel critically important.

Third, leaders perceive pay to be generally less dominant in employees' negotiations compared to five or ten years ago; instead, people are prioritizing learning opportunities, career progression, and flexibility. Similarly to mortgages, people see drawbacks to fixing their terms too tightly today if they are looking to maximize possibilities or take advantage of unexpected developments over the longer term. This chimes with research showing that while half of us would like higher salaries, only 16% of the time[2] pay is the primary reason people leave.

Finally, leaders are united on the pitfalls of leading with compensation. Pay deals and decisions have to be seen as fair, equitable, and competitive (within the context of the full package of pay and benefits) but if you take a pay-led approach, employees will only stay for as long as your offer exceeds your competitors' offers. Plus, by simply focusing on the financials you're not helping people to visualize a compelling future at your company and so the haggling over pay will pop up at every review point.

2. Flexibility

If pay gets people over the threshold, flexibility keeps them under your roof. This was a pre-pandemic top five priority for people, and is now a deal-breaker. In 2024, we witnessed some rolling back of post-pandemic flexibility from the likes of investment banks and technology firms including Goldman Sachs, Meta, and Zoom however looking at how turnover rates for different models of work have changed over the past few years, it is clear that turnover has risen more sharply for the office-only model compared to remote and hybrid models, with the latter showing the lowest rate of turnover (see Figure 2).

Figure 2 Turnover rates by work model[3]

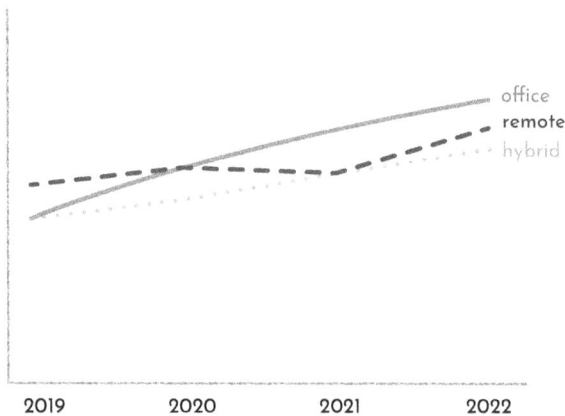

| | 2019 | 2020 | 2021 | 2022 |

This is consistent with how prospective and current employees are landing decisions about whether to join, stay with or leave their organization:

	Job candidates	Current employees
When flexibility is offered:	Are more interested in the role	Are more loyal
When flexibility is inadequate or lacking:	Are more likely to decline a job offer	Are more likely to leave

3. Interesting work

This is about intellectually stimulating work that provides us with opportunities to grow professionally and acquire new skills. It's also about the absence of soul-sapping bureaucracy, politics, and other sources of organizational friction that get in the way of doing – and enjoying – our day job. Contrary to the popular characterization of Gen Z[‡] obsessing about learning opportunities, most of us want these too; in his book, *Drive*, Daniel Pink pinpoints mastery as one of our three intrinsic motivators. A culture that values learning and growth is critical for retention; according to the professional networking and jobs site LinkedIn, a majority of employees stay longer with companies that provide regular professional development opportunities.[4] One law firm leader expressed this personally to me:

> I've always loved learning and going beyond my role. I've been curious about other areas of the business and what makes people tick. I have been lucky to work with people who trust me and have allowed me to play to my strengths.

Through thick and thin

Loyalty cannot be demanded or instantly given, it can only be created over a period of time through a relationship of consistent,

‡ Born between 1997 and 2012.

reciprocal trust and respect. As social beings, we are hard-wired to seek mutually beneficial group relationships. Our desire for affinity is just as profound in the world of work as in our home lives; for 73% of us, having a meaningful connection with our colleagues is one of the most important things about our job.[5]

When we feel that sense of community, we're likely to describe it as 'being there for each other' and we are more likely to stay even if other aspects of the job are less than ideal. We place a high-value on working with others towards a worthwhile goal, particularly when the shared beliefs and behaviours align with our own interests and world view. However, leaders have found it challenging to nurture that powerful close-knit feel as remote- and hybrid-working have proliferated.

Compounding this is the fact that people tend to be loyal to an individual first and an organization second. So, when a trusted colleague – a sponsor, a mentor, someone who has looked after us in the past, someone to whom we can reveal our vulnerabilities – moves on and later offers us an opportunity, we're more minded to join them.

Scouting around

Two questions employers would love to know the answers to are: how many of their people are looking to leave at any one point in time, and who? Broader research on this doesn't offer reassuring answers:[6]

1. In the UK and the US, roughly one in two employees are open to, or actively considering, leaving their organization, the highest ratio of the past decade.
2. Across Europe, the ratio is slightly lower at one in three.
3. Across the global workforce, one in every 20 employees is *actively disengaged*, meaning they don't support their employers' goals and they're not committed to their role there.

There are certain points in the employee lifecycle when the flight risk is highest:

- *The first 100 days.* Most people make up their minds about a new job within their first month and for a significant number, within their first week.
- *Mid-career.* After 7–15 years into our careers, we've acquired valuable skills and experience and we're hungry for momentum, a combination that makes us more poachable.
- *Moments that matter.* When a critical life- or work-related event or experience happens, people weigh up their organization's response and decide how they feel about it.

Certain groups of employees are more likely to head voluntarily for the door, these are younger employees, parents, shorter-tenure employees,[7] and women. Millennials entering the workforce since 2010 stay on average just over one year, compared to nearly six years for those who started work in the 1960s. This isn't just down to flightier attitudes: they've faced higher youth unemployment, higher job insecurity, and less predictable work volumes and contracts. Women are only slightly less likely to leave than men; this gap has significantly reduced in the past two decades due to rises in the number of dual-career couples and national retirement ages.

Why people leave

Switching voluntarily from staying put to saying goodbye is rarely a flash decision thanks in part to a cognitive bias known as the sunk cost fallacy where we stick with an unsatisfactory situation even when moving would clearly be more beneficial because we've substantially invested in our current set-up. It's only when our frustration or needs reach a tipping point that we conclude it's time to go. The following factors regularly crop up as the straws that break the camel's back:[¶]

¶ An idiom rooted in Arabic culture and sprinkled liberally in literature across the centuries, it illustrates the idea of a cumulative set of issues building up to a tipping point.

1. *Toxic work cultures:* Where people don't feel it is safe to speak up honestly and where bullying behaviours exist. Research into 2022s so-called Great Resignation found that a toxic corporate culture is by far the strongest predictor of attrition and ten times more important than compensation.[8] In client research I've conducted, former employees have commented how no-one dared to question deadlines or speak up about any difficulties or challenges.

2. *Restructurings and layoffs:* These trigger more voluntary exits with a high proportion of employers recognizing this as the top reason people choose to leave. Layoffs have the strongest and most immediate effects on voluntary turnover compared to performance/misconduct dismissals and voluntary departures.[9] Small wonder then that the trend for quiet layoffs grew during 2024 although this approach can backfire, as global consulting firm PwC discovered. They instructed departing employees to leave covertly by not disclosing their redundancies to their colleagues and by sticking to a predefined response if asked, however this guidance was leaked and hit the headlines.

3. *Overwork and overload:* Greedy jobs are those where we are rewarded for long hours and being constantly available to our employer. Doing the job well isn't sufficient, people tell me, they are frequently exhorted to keep 'doing more'. One exhausted leaver admitted 'it was 110% all the time and you just can't keep that up'. Women are disproportionately impacted by greedy jobs because they tend to shoulder more of the domestic and caring responsibilities at home; little surprise then that the volume of work is the top gender-related factor swaying women when deciding to leave their job.[10] Younger workers are also discouraged by greedy jobs, and they are significantly less motivated to do more than required compared to their organizational leaders.

4. *Stuck and overlooked*: People often leave when their career trajectory has stalled. They might progress at first then end up frozen indefinitely at a certain level for no clear reason; this has been documented to particularly impact those from lower socio-economic or non-professional backgrounds. Feeling deprioritized pushes people to leave, particularly if they had previously benefitted from being in the spotlight, forming part of a favoured group or being chosen for select development opportunities. Others feel disadvantaged by so-called 'diversity hires and promotions'.

5. *Not trusted*: When an individual's expertise and contribution isn't recognized or when career-enhancing exposure is withheld, retention takes a hit. Firm-wide RTO (return to office) mandates send a strong subtext that 'we don't trust you'; aggrieved leavers say, 'I was never given the opportunity to present my work to senior colleagues' and 'they never listened to my point of view as an expert employed to do the job'.

6. *Underperformance*: When a line manager has been managing an underperforming individual appropriately and transparently, it can often result in the individual choosing to leave ahead of a likely dismissal on performance grounds.

7. *External factors*: When life throws a curve ball, workers can reasonably expect their employer to explore any adjustments in order to retain them. However, there are limits as employers are mindful of setting unrealistic precedents and ensuring equity across the workforce.

8. *Technology*: Some groups perceive AI as an opportunity, others as a threat. Those aged under 55 are more excited about its potential impact on their career compared to those aged 55 and over. Nearly 70% who fear AI are actively looking for a new job.[11]

Advice for leaders

How confident are you that you know why people stay with or leave your organization? Below are recommendations for how you can gather reliable data and mine it for valuable retention insights. Bear in mind that it's how you *respond* to what you learn that will have the biggest impact, so take meaningful action and signal this clearly.

1. *Conduct 1:1 stay interviews (or focus groups)* either with a representative cross-section of your workforce or with people who you suspect may be more likely to leave and/ or harder to replace. Note that in the UK, you cannot legally ask an employee if they are planning to stay or leave so your stay interview questions should be focused on understanding better their current experiences, motivations, and concerns.

2. *Ensure exit interviews are always conducted*, preferably by HR or someone other than the leaver's line manager; share an interview guide for consistency and thoroughness and collate the feedback.

3. *Invite an external facilitator to conduct research among recent leavers* to understand what made them leave and what would have persuaded them to stay.

4. *Include questions in regular pulse surveys* such as 'would you recommend our organization to a friend?', 'what do you value most about working here?', and 'what one thing would you change about our organization?'.

5. *Encourage managers to hold regular 1:1 meetings with direct reports* to informally recognize their contributions, agree priorities, and surface any issues. Employees who have meaningful weekly conversations with their managers are four times more likely to feel engaged than those who don't.[12]

6. *Hold a townhall meeting* where there's a slot for PMQ-style[§] open questions with unscripted answers from leaders.
7. *Analyse your employee tenure and turnover data* to identify trends by level, function and diversity characteristics and any attrition hotspots.
8. *Use conjoint analysis to evaluate what aspects of their work different employees value the most and least;* forcing them to make trade-offs or rank them avoids unrealistic wish lists.

Advice for individuals

Use the following traffic-light framework to bring more intentionality into your own decisions about staying or moving on.

Green	1. Thinking about your current role and organization, what are your important boxes to tick if you want to feel enthusiastic about your future there? 2. What opportunities would you say yes to? 3. Where's your ideal position in the golden triangle?
Amber	1. What warning signs would nudge you to review your situation? 2. Who could you speak to about these? 3. What are you noticing about the opportunities available to your peers and colleagues and their general progress compared to your own?
Red	1. Decide in advance what your 'red lines' or 'quit criteria' are and include a timeframe. 2. Network internally and externally, chat with recruiters and educate yourself about your market value and where the opportunities are. 3. Actively keep an attractive Plan B on the table at all times, both inside and outside of your current employer.

[§] PMQs are where the UK Prime Minister faces questions in Parliament on any aspect of the Government's agenda. They happen weekly on Wednesdays when Parliament is in session.

The modern battleground

In this chapter you've seen how people will stay when (broadly) their job provides a sufficient level of remuneration, stimulating work alongside supportive colleagues, and the ability to tailor their working time and location to suit. But none of these factors is a constant anymore: function by function, individual by individual, there's a much more complex relationship with what keeps people in play today compared to a decade or so ago. This is the era of individualization and businesses need to reflect this in their offer to employees and the day-to-day experience. For as you'll see next, retaining skilled employees is critical for business survival and growth. In the continued war for talent, the victors are the 'stickiest' organizations.

Chapter 3
Why retention matters

'Love, if I weep it will not matter,
And if you laugh I shall not care.'

Edna St. Vincent Millay

Retention reigns

WHEN LEADERS FIND themselves awake at night pondering pressing business issues, retention is likely to be headlining the list. Here's why:

	However: 60% of employers find it a challenge to attract and retain the talent they need.[2]
Their top operational priority – even above revenue generation – is about retaining their talent.[1]	
	And: Over 90% of HR leaders are concerned about employee turnover and retention.[3]

In this chapter, I'll explore how retention challenges have been changing over the past couple of decades and why retention has become such a thorny issue for employers, and I'll chart some of the pressing financial consequences of raised employee turnover. The benefits of holding onto your skilled employees aren't purely financial but multi-faceted, with prized commercial and operational advantages too. Towards the end of this chapter is some advice for leaders to guide you in diagnosing your organization's retention risks and for individuals to help you explore your own personal motivations around your career decisions.

Upheaval on a grand scale

COVID-19 was a seismic global event that exploded previously accepted work norms and forced companies to redesign in lightning-fast timescales the way work was delivered and how we communicated and collaborated with one another. In parallel, the curtailment of our personal freedoms and connections during lockdowns provoked deep reflection and reassessment by many about what mattered most in our lives and what we wanted from our work. We discovered life without a daily commute on overcrowded, expensive and unreliable public transport or in clogged rush-hour traffic, the joy (ahem!) of being able to fit life admin into our working day, and unprecedented levels of wellbeing support from our employers. Since the world re-opened, there has been some recent, partial rolling back of flexibility in certain industries (more on this later); however, most employers acknowledge the ground has shifted irrevocably and the long-term winners will be those who fully explore, embrace, and exploit the post-pandemic landscape of work.

But retention challenges today aren't just the legacy of the COVID-19 pandemic; they have emerged as a result of other trends too. Ageing populations and falling birth rates around the world along with delayed national retirement ages have reshaped the age contours of the global workforce: across the OECD (the Organisation for Economic Co-operation and Development, whose membership is comprised of 38 predominantly rich western countries) the proportion of 55–64 year olds in work is 66% and rising inexorably.[4] This places a dual pressure on employers to tailor the flexibility and benefits to this older cohort and to identify how to replace their expanding number of retirees – the biggest workforce conundrum for 30% of CEOs in the UK.[5]

Another massive shift has been women's increased participation in the workforce. Within one generation social attitudes, employment legislation, and support for working parents have evolved enormously. When my mother, now in her eighties, married my father in the late 1960s, she had no choice but to resign from the globe-trotting job she loved as a cabin crew member for BOAC airline due to their policies. I have continued to work through marriage and parenthood as one half of a 'DCC' (dual career couple), the model that now dominates in many countries. Yet women still face unresolved gender barriers at work that impede their job satisfaction, wellbeing and career advancement. Employers haven't cracked the 'gender agenda', as evidenced by the still-leaky female pipeline of talent, stubborn gender pay gaps, and the widespread gender imbalance in leadership roles.

A third trend is the rise of job 'nomadacy' whereby employees change jobs and companies more often. We're getting pickier: 62% of candidates only apply for roles that meet most of their requirements,[6] and we'll move sooner if we're not satisfied: people who rate their employers only two out of five stars on Glassdoor are nearly twice as likely to apply elsewhere compared to five star raters.[7] Younger people typically move more frequently, with those entering the workforce since 2010 averaging just over one year per role compared to nearly six years for those who started work in the 1960s.[8]

A fourth factor is the insufficient supply of skilled workers to meet current and future demand. The talent pond that businesses are fishing in simply isn't well-stocked enough. Across all sectors in the UK, this skills gap is widening and currently stands at an 18-year high of 80% according to ManpowerGroup, the third largest staffing firm in the world. Globally, 54% of companies report talent shortages and nearly nine in ten executives cite imminent skills gaps.[9] No wonder UK bosses place almost as much priority on investing in skills as making capital investments.

Compounding this, technology is fast reconfiguring job design and careers: jobs that exist today won't exist tomorrow and the converse is also true. The OECD estimates that 1.1 billion jobs are likely to be fundamentally recast by technology in the next decade and to meet the shortfall business leaders everywhere are looking to upskill and re-skill existing employees to meet their future resourcing needs. This has consequences for us as individuals too: one in 16 of us globally may need to switch our occupation by 2030 to stand a chance of getting hooked by a recruiter.

Money walks

When you lose a valued employee, it hurts your business and every departure adds pressure to your bottom line. Why? Because the cost of replacing those employees is expensive. Assessments of exactly *how* expensive tend to vary, in part because it depends on employee seniority and pay grade, the availability or scarcity of those skills in the market and the efficiency of your recruitment process. Re-filling individual roles can cost from 40% of annual salary for frontline workers to 200% for managers and leaders, with technical experts not far behind the latter.[10] That's at the individual employee level; what does this add up to for the business over the course of a full year? Let's apply some simple mathematics based on the average turnover rate for UK workers of 35%[11] (this varies by industry) and an assumption that the replacement cost per individual is 100% of salary. A business that has 100 employees with an average annual salary of £50,000 could be shelling out £1.75 million per year in employee turnover costs – and a substantial proportion of those exits could have been prevented. Ouch.

These turnover costs include direct hiring expenses (agency and headhunter fees plus the cumulative cost of HR professionals, leaders, and senior managers giving up their time to interview candidates) and the indirect costs of lost productivity while the role remains vacant and as the new joiner gradually gets up to speed in their role. It's in the business' interests to rehire quickly but recruitment processes are often lengthy and/or unsuccessful: in the UK it takes on average 40 days to hire a new employee. Plus, as the CEO of a leading British property development company observed to me 'it's time-consuming recruiting somebody and then inducting them into the business and settling them into a team. You have a tail-off of productivity before the leaver exits then a gradual ramp up with the new joiner; for senior roles that can equate to 12 months of reduced productivity. You can't do that too often'.

Another way to consider the financial impact of employee turnover is to look at the return on investment that is being lost. According to the UK's Department for Education, British employers invest around £42 billion per year in training and developing their workforce, averaging out at £1,530 per employee, per annum. That hypothetical 100-employee business is seeing £53,550 of their annual training budget go to waste or benefit another employer.

An era, not eternity

Retention is more nuanced than simply counting heads: as leaders, you don't just want people to stay, you're after their drive and discretionary effort too. You want a committed workforce who are focused on delivering to the best of their ability and 'making it happen'. You don't want people to be coasting along comfortably or 'quiet quitters', aka workers who are staying in role but putting in minimal effort.

There's also the sensitive reality that you don't necessarily want everyone to stay forever. It's ok for certain groups to stay just for an era rather than eternity, and some turnover is healthy and beneficial so that you are bringing in new ideas and new ways of working. Fresh faces can bring fresh thinking and dynamism to complement the views of longer-serving employees whose perspectives may have narrowed over time.

Setting aside the question of specific skills and knowledge, individuals who fall into one or more of the following three categories will be particularly valuable to your business:

1. Those who have undergone the most significant amount of change in the shortest amount of time, because they become immensely influential in encouraging others to embrace change too.
2. Those who have helped to build or shape the organization because they're typically more professionally and emotionally invested and likely to understand the future plan.
3. The high performers, because these deliver four times the value to the business than average-performing colleagues.

Crafting enticing roles, career paths, and experiences of work for these 'most wanted' employees pays off by helping you to mitigate or circumvent some of the financial challenges described above that will otherwise add to your costs and eat up your profits. It also engenders a range of commercial and operational benefits that contribute to top line growth.

Reasons to be cheerful

Here are four ways in which increased retention and lower employer turnover benefits your business.

1. It aids competitive advantage

When you're a leader, you're looking at the business through two lenses, one internally focused and the other externally focused. With the internal focus, you're making continuous incremental improvements to keep your business attractive to current and future talent in the short-term. With the external focus, you're keeping a watchful eye on the market and assessing what your competitors are doing. As the COO of a specialist insurance group explained 'you're worrying about the "here and now" and at the same time you're also trying to get 12–24 months ahead of your competitors'.

Retaining skilled, valuable employees helps you to build stronger relationships with your clients, which is unanimously seen by executives as a source of competitive advantage. When you have colleagues with excellent interpersonal and relationship skills, you have happier clients because they are receiving a top-notch service and the client relationship is being well-tended. Happy clients come back to you next time they have a need because they have built a relationship of trust with the individuals who are looking after them.

Holding onto your global, diverse talent also enhances your competitive advantage by facilitating your access into different markets, helping you to launch new products and services successfully in new geographies and responding to local nuances in client and customer behaviour. Clients often want to see diversity in your organization; in professional services, a homogenous team can jeopardize your chances of success in a competitive client opportunity and in general, customers may turn to an alternative player if they feel your business doesn't sufficiently represent them or their interests. This is borne out by research published in the *Harvard Business Review* which found that companies with more diverse teams are 45% more likely to report market growth and 70% more likely to capture new markets.[12]

2. It positions you to meet future business needs

In a growing business, it's not good enough to have what you had yesterday, you have to have a better business tomorrow.

> We need to be the most attractive company in our field for talent and we need to retain all of the talent that we've got within the organization – not achieving this is the largest single impediment to our growth.

This perspective from the UK Managing Director of a global construction materials supplier illustrates how critical retention is to achieving your medium- to longer-term business goals.

Retaining employees allows you to look at ways in which you can move people within and across functions to respond to changing demand. You can quickly reallocate resource to an area that is overstretched and under pressure; you can bring together spot teams to explore new opportunities without having to set up a costly or inflexible permanent structure.

While some employees you want to keep will inevitably decide to move on sooner than you'd like, with an eye on future business needs you can welcome back 'boomerangs' (former employees) to your mutual advantage. This can form a deliberate part of your talent strategy; savvy businesses carefully nurture relationships with former employees through alumni networks, marketing events, and other channels. If and when some of these employees decide to return to your business, they bring with them valuable expertise that they have gained in the meantime, plus you are hiring a known quantity who knows you in return and who is motivated to pursue a second career chapter with you.

3. It increases your efficiency and resilience

Higher retention rates have a multiplier effect in operational and performance terms. As well as reducing operating costs, low turnover also benefits other aspects of business performance: it increases morale, strengthens loyalty and interpersonal connections, enhances the employee experience, and results in higher levels of motivation and job satisfaction.

All of these positive outcomes add to your operational stability and your ability to weather external shocks such as political changes and economic downturns. A stable, skilled workforce is also less vulnerable to disruptions from technological innovation. These consequences directly benefit your employees, so you are in essence creating a powerful virtual circle that works for both you and for your team.

4. It offers long-term productivity gains

In response to the insufficient supply of skills in the external market, many businesses are opting to 'grow their own' by retraining existing employees, often through very ambitious, large-scale initiatives involving tens of thousands, and even hundreds of thousands, of workers globally. Many professionals are receptive to these opportunities, seeing them as strengthening their prospects for stable, long-term employment in the future, and they are open to learning new skills or completely retraining in order to remain attractive in the jobs market.[13] The virtuous circle plays out again here as companies with strong learning cultures typically enjoy higher rates of retention, more internal mobility, and a more robust talent pipeline compared to those organizations with weaker learning cultures.[14]

From head to heart

So far in this chapter, the case I've set out for why retention matters has largely focused on rational, commercial arguments. I've been appealing to your 'head' and to your business' bottom line, but there's another angle too which, for me, speaks more directly to your 'heart' and to the soul of your organization.

I acknowledge that a degree of career mobility undoubtedly opens up choices for people and simultaneously contributes to the continuous healthy replenishment of the labour market – I'm not in favour of a wholesale return to jobs for life. However, I passionately believe in the value of retention for the reasons below, with the starting assumption that the work cultures people are operating in are healthy and nurturing, not toxic ones.

1. It allows people to spread their wings and take career leaps and risks without resorting to the more drastic step of switching employers or setting up on their own in the wobbly hope that the grass is greener on the other side.
2. It gives people greater security, enabling them to grow in confidence and to plan with confidence inside and outside of work, which in turn benefits their families and communities too.
3. It offers the opportunity to forge deeper, more fulfilling relationships with colleagues and clients that can endure across career lifetimes, rather than transactional and fleeting ones that are quietly extinguished the day someone leaves.

In short, improved retention holds out the promise of a mutually beneficial symbiotic relationship between an individual and the business they work for, each enabling the other to realize latent potential, achieve breakthroughs, and make the seemingly impossible happen. Multiplied across every business and every country, the force for good that this can bring to our world is exciting beyond words, capable of transforming intractable and complex challenges into lasting, enriching solutions.

Advice for leaders

In *Wilful Blindness*, business leader Margaret Heffernan shows how our inattention to early warning signs leaves us dangerously susceptible to organizational failures and disasters. With the proverb 'forewarned is forearmed' in mind, here are eight ways to diagnose your retention risks before they imperil your business:

1. *Know how you stack up.* Compare your current retention rate versus the industry average; are you weaker or stronger on this than your competitors?
2. *Chart your workforce profile.* Calculate the spread of your workforce across age and gender bands; how exposed is it to higher turnover risks at different life stages?
3. *Analyse your vacancy stats.* Identify the hardest roles to fill or skills to find; what are you doing proactively to remedy this in the short- and longer-term?
4. *Look after your 'most wanted'.* Plot your high performers, influential change agents and the highly invested; how are they feeling about their future in your organization?
5. *Don't lose them before they've joined.* Find out what your recruitment approach is like from candidates who've been through it; what's putting people off?
6. *Crunch the numbers.* Use some of the statistics from earlier in this chapter to model the full financial impact of your employee turnover rate; how does this affect your bottom line?
7. *Do some hand-holding.* Invest extra effort in helping hard-to-recruit new joiners to get going with confidence and ease; have their managers got a plan for their first 100 days?
8. *Think the unthinkable.* Sketch out your retention 'worst case' scenarios; what signals would flag up these risks early enough to allow you to stem the outflow?

Advice for individuals

One of my podcast guests thoughtfully commented that 'careers make sense looking backwards'. To bring more intentionality into your career path from here onwards, use these five prompts to explore your own personal motivations:

1. What do you need to be successful in your work?
2. What can you take from your current role to make yourself more valuable to your current employer?

3. What can you take from external interests and responsibilities?

4. In your present role, how can you 'build your skills, not your resumé', as Sheryl Sandberg, former COO of Facebook (now Meta) puts it.

5. How can you combine your skills in creative ways to open up potential new options work-wise?

Stick around

In Part 1, you've discovered what makes organizations 'sticky' and the role that People Glue plays in a business' ability to be successful over the longer-term. I have set out the factors that persuade people to stay and those that make them walk away, and why achieving good levels of retention is simultaneously challenging and critical for business leaders.

While businesses are seeking better retention, workers are seeking more freedom. Part 2 turns to the other half of this paradox – freedom – that lies at the heart of the employer-employee relationship. What are we really talking about here? How has freedom evolved over the decades and what kinds of freedom are employees asking for today? I'll look in depth at what freedom means to different people and what limits or boundaries employers should be placing – and are placing – on our freedom at work, and why. Part 2 also offers a first glimpse of the four freedoms that matter most (explored more fully in Part 3) and the internal and external forces that constrain employers and reduce our work freedom.

Part 2
Freedom
at work

'If you love something, set it free. If it comes back, it is yours. If it doesn't, it never was.'

Unknown

Chapter 4
Freedom unpicked

'Let's agree on the mountain peak we're aiming for, then be open to the possible trails we'll take to get there.'

Anonymous

The starting point

WHEN WE'RE TALKING about freedom at work, to what are we referring? To a certain extent there is a subjective element at play: one person might take a very narrow view, another a more expansive one; a third might consider it in conceptual terms and a fourth, its practical manifestations. If you want to retain your valued employees by offering them more freedom, then a critical first step is to define and agree what *your organization* means by freedom; only after that can you confidently articulate this to others and build it into your organization's set-up and ways of working.

The following pages offer guidance about what freedom at work *is* and what it *isn't*. You'll discover the four core elements of freedom that people are searching for and that are critical for creating a 'sticky' organization. I'll share my own research findings about what the four freedoms mean to people, how they've typically experienced these in their own careers and what impact a lack of freedom has had on them – their motivation, their performance, their career decisions. I'll explain why freedom is a two-way commitment not a one-sided affair, and how you can frame the deal you're offering about freedom in your organization.

Power, baby

In researching People Glue, I was struck by how many leaders drew on the analogy of parenting when discussing freedom at work. 'One of life's great paradoxes is that in order to raise safe, healthy, resilient children, we have to set them free', mused a CEO who is the mother of two daughters. We have to gradually equip them to take independent steps and decisions as they progressively explore the world without us; 'helicopter parenting', where parents hover constantly and swoop in to intervene at every opportunity, results in a less confident, clingier child.

Anita Cleare, a leading UK parenting expert and author of *The Work/Parent Switch*, explains the developmental psychology at play: 'freedom is actually a handover of power: what leaders are giving to their employees is the power to make certain decisions in whatever way they choose.' For Anita, there are three critical components to a successful handover:

1. An *open conversation* upfront about the freedom on offer, where both parties talk through mutual concerns and agree their approach.
2. A *managed transfer* of power comprising a series of steps towards the desired outcome with checkpoints along the way.
3. A *process of discovery* whereby both parties learn from failure and how to get it right next time.

Transactional analysis is another psychological parenting-related framework; it proposes three different roles that we consciously or unconsciously adopt in our interactions with others: parent (authority figure), child (compliant or otherwise), or adult (rational and objective). Organizations where parent-child dynamics abound will find it harder to offer freedom successfully, whereas organizations that promote adult-adult modes of operating and communicating will be better positioned.

What freedom is

When it comes to the concept of freedom at work, the following perspectives echo consistently across all my conversations with leaders. Freedom is:

- *Clarity* throughout the organization about *what* you're trying to achieve, from your overarching mission statement to your business objectives, through to every individual knowing their role and why they're doing it, and it goes deeply into your business processes.
- A shared *mindset* about *how* you're moving towards your goals. Your role as a leader is to explain the direction of travel that you're going in and some collective behaviours that you hold yourselves to; you're setting out some clear parameters within which people are empowered to act, and if necessary ask for forgiveness, not permission. You're not dictating a path for people to obediently follow but encouraging people to figure this out together and to do this successfully, you have to create an environment where people can confidently explore different paths that they haven't been down before, or do a deep dive in a new area.
- *Subjective* and nuanced, where one person's freedom is another person's neglect. For example, some will be happy to wing it and feel hemmed in by a prescriptive environment, whereas others will prefer to operate in

a more tightly defined structure and find ambiguity frustrating. Freedom might also look different for different teams, depending on the line of business and the team's function and this may be reflected in varying policies and benefits packages for say shift-based, office-based, and site-based employees.

- *Best partnered with support.* This isn't about throwing someone in and expecting them to swim. Returning to Anita's parenting advice, coaching those less confident with freedom involves trial runs, halfway houses, and gradual progression. Finding out what's important for each individual is critical but this can feel effortful and a 'time suck' for managers; similarly having all those power transactions and micro-debates about control is quite tiring for leaders.

- A *journey* that starts from a secure base and comes with an emergency helpline. People have got to be on the journey that you want them to be on. At the same time, while you're letting people get on with it and make their own decisions, they need to be able to press the red button when something goes wrong. That red button is leaders' governance over the major issues that could jeopardize the business.

What freedom isn't

Sometimes a certain proposition can be enticingly portrayed as a freedom but is in reality a wolf in sheep's clothing. Watch out for the following false, sharp-toothed freedoms:

- *An enticing-sounding philosophy devoid of any rigour or structure.* This just results in a general fogginess that gets the business nowhere. You run the risk of a lot of people having no idea what they're supposed to be doing, teams or functions that are operating sub-optimally, and gridlock and confusion in work processes that flow across multiple teams.

- A *completely hands-off attitude*. People need to know they're applying their efforts to work that matters and see how they can progress career-wise. Allowing complete agency without any direction or support can spectacularly backfire when the individual feels anxious or angry about being left to sink or swim. A group executive at a leading real estate consultancy explained 'we want to give people the confidence to do the job effectively without fear and we work very hard on that because everybody's different'.

- *Exploitation*. At the extreme, behind promises of freedom can lurk a harsh callousness by greedy employers who take full advantage of the power imbalance, for example offering one-sided zero hours contracts on low pay with unpredictable work volumes, or in higher pay contexts, demanding a hardcore work ethic, exceptional performance and relentlessly long hours.

- *A self-governing free-for-all*. Offering freedom isn't about saying yes to everything or indulging people's individual ambitions above the organization's raison d'être. Employees have to share, debate, and act as a team. What can also feel awkward for you as a leader is when somebody senior on your team is pushing for absolute freedom to do what they want; often what they are actually making a bid for is unfettered control.

- *Unnecessary division*. Sometimes a certain freedom sounds forward-thinking and workable but subsequently reveals unexpected downsides. One very successful newer player in the financial planning industry trialled unlimited annual leave which proved highly popular with some but caused a shift-scheduling enigma for others, resulting in a two-tier system of freedom which, according to their CEO, was worse than not having it in the first place.

- *An unwillingness to listen.* For you to do your job effectively
as a leader, you need live, honest feedback from the front
line and understanding why a decision or a new initiative
doesn't work as intended is business-critical. The CEO of
a specialty insurance business encourages people to call
him on 'the stupid phone' if a new centrally-developed
policy or proposal needs amending to work effectively in
their part of the business.

The four freedoms

Let's get granular and unpack freedom in more practical terms.
Freedom at work comprises the following four elements.

1. Autonomy

This is the freedom to manage your work and working
arrangements in a way that enables you to deliver at your best.
In part, this is about when and where you work and the formal
and/or informal flexibility you enjoy. It's also about how you
choose to get your work done, being trusted to determine
your priorities, being able to influence decisions, and not being
micromanaged. Finally, it's freedom *from* work, being able (and
encouraged) to disconnect regularly, and for work not to be
all-consuming.

2. Growth

This is the freedom to enhance your skills, develop in an exciting
direction and grow your career. It's being empowered to think, be
creative, and get resourceful, where you can contribute 'outside
the box' and implement your ideas. Growth is also the freedom
to expand your skillset, reflect on your work experiences, and
integrate these into your own learning so that you can move

forwards rather than stagnate. Part of this is also about having the freedom to associate with others to help you grow a valuable professional network. Finally, growth is the freedom to curate your career, whether you're following up a well-trodden route or exploring a more squiggly path, and to access support from your employer along the way.

3. Self-expression

This is the freedom to be yourself, to speak up in a psychologically safe culture, to express your personality and be accepted for who you are. You're able to bring your mind and spirit to the work rather than just keep the seat warm. You don't feel compelled to mask your true self or 'pass' and you feel like you belong. Everyone's ideas are welcome regardless of role, all jobs are considered equally important, and there's no hierarchy dictating who gets to speak or be listened to. People are free from the fear of reproach or reprisal when discussing workplace dynamics or negotiating your worth.

4. Meaningful work

This is the freedom to focus on the important work, invest your working hours productively, and make a positive impact. Instead of getting bogged down in bureaucracy, friction, politics, or the daily grind, you've got freedom to operate. It's ok to say no to pointless meetings, unnecessary work, non-promotable tasks, and when new responsibilities are added to your plate, something else is taken off. You're not caught up in endless power plays or yet another change for change's sake; you're able to pursue the work you're passionate about (within the context of your role), make an impact and leave a legacy.

In Part 3, I'll do a deeper dive into each of these four freedoms; for now, bear in mind that it's not about choosing one over another. As one CEO summed up to me: 'the most powerful glue lies at the intersection of these four freedoms'.

Freedom stories

In researching this book, my colleague Eliana Strauss and I conducted a short survey inviting people to tell us what freedom at work meant to them. We asked participants:

1. To rank the four freedoms in order of *importance* to them personally.
2. The extent to which they had *experienced* each of those freedoms in their work to date.
3. What *impact* these four freedoms – or the lack of them – had had on them and their career.

The responses and stories shared by the 67 people who generously responded were insightful and often poignant.

In terms of the relative *importance* of the four freedoms, across all responses and demographics the ranking emerged as follows:

1st	Autonomy	Over half rated this as most important with few attaching low importance to it.
2nd	Meaningful work	This was rarely ranked as a top priority, and a few ranked it as least important.
3rd	Self-expression	This was evenly distributed across the rankings, nudging into third place overall.
4th	Growth	While ranked lowest overall, views on this were quite polarised; see more on this in Chapter 8.

Turning now to the question of which freedoms people had typically *experienced* or otherwise, the ranking remains the same as for *importance* with some conclusions emerging as follows:

1st	Autonomy	While highest ranked overall, again responses were quite polarized, and a significant number ranked this lowest.
2nd	Meaningful work	Many found purpose in their work but didn't necessarily see this as their dominant workplace freedom.
3rd	Self-expression	While some individuals felt free to be themselves at work, a significant portion said they lacked full psychological safety.
4th	Growth	Many respondents still faced barriers to career and skill advancement.

In Part 3, I'll reveal how both *importance* and *experience* scores varied across different demographic groups. Interestingly, progressing into a leadership role didn't necessarily improve people's experiences of the four freedoms, and a number of people commented that they felt their individual experiences tended to be more positive when they matched the majority demographic in their organization rather than belonging to an under-represented group.

The following comments illustrate how many people have encountered the say–do gap that exists around freedom, even in organizations with admirable goals, and how they've had to consciously engineer more freedom for themselves:

Many companies talk a big game about these kind of freedoms but very few deliver because they don't trust their employees and don't invest in employee happiness.

I feel I've been lucky to experience all of these significantly, in part due to the fact I will change roles if I can't, or take on extra projects that allow me to do this.

I've spent a lot of time with companies wanting you to conform to a 'type'… finding an employer where you can be accepted with your true personality brings the best out of you.

A noble cause is no guarantee to experiencing freedom at work.

In terms of the *impact* that freedom, or its absence, has on individuals and their careers:

- *People's accounts bear testimony to how the positive impacts of work-related freedom ripple far and wide.* It makes work more enjoyable, it encourages innovative thinking, it helps people to manage competing demands, it contributes to better mental health – in short, people flourish. This in turn generates other desirable consequences: people put in discretionary effort, give more back to others, are less likely to drop out when faced with home-life challenges and ultimately, the business reaps the benefit too with higher levels of productivity, more motivated, innovative employees and a more stable workforce: 'it's a real win for me *and* the business', which is 'fundamentally important if a business wants to stay fit for the future'.

- *The consequences when freedom is limited or denied are deep and wide-ranging.* When people don't feel able to do their best work or see any way to progress, their work gradually loses meaning, they end up doing the bare minimum and become disengaged and resentful. Not feeling heard or trusted to deliver chips away at their confidence and motivation, they stop speaking up and start 'giving answers which managers expect to hear'. They question their own ability and their commitment to the organization. This downward spiral damages the business as performance plummets, collaboration contracts, and more employees head for the exit. One person described this as 'suffocating. I got the hell out'.

First among equals

When ranking the four freedoms in terms of importance, people shared differing thought processes and conclusions. For some, all four carried near-equal weight: 'it was difficult to rank these as they are all important to me and I wouldn't stay in a role if I didn't feel I had these.' For others, a waterfall logic applied, for example:

> If first and foremost I can't be myself and feel safe [self-expression] then that's a 'no'. Assuming I can 'be me' then I want to be able to work in a way that I can do my best work [autonomy]. Assuming I can do that, then the work I do has to mean something, I want to make a difference [meaningful work]. *If all those three are true*, then growth is a natural product.

Another person took the view that 'humans are good at bringing meaning to their work *if other factors are met*'. A third group of respondents differentiated between freedoms they saw as deal-breakers versus 'nice-to-haves': 'I consider psychological safety a non-negotiable, to the point where I probably wouldn't be in the organization if it wasn't there'.

Alongside any conclusions we draw from this small sample, we should bear in mind at all times that people work in different ways and are most productive at different times. So, they will also value different weightings and applications of these four freedoms. As one respondent warned '[I] appreciate [there's] a need to operate across some core hours and in-person meetings but a rigid one-size-fits-all approach is *not* the future'. This is because our priorities typically change depending on our life stage; for example, 'I love my job and the work I do but it has to work for me and my family'. Additionally, our needs and motivations alter over the years as we notch up career experiences, ascend to more influential positions and hopefully become more financially secure: 'the order has changed and evolved as my career has progressed.'

Advice for leaders

If I were to individually ask leaders in your organization to describe the freedom deal on offer to your employees, how confidently and consistently would they all answer this? And what about employees? If you're unsure, try it and see what emerges.

If your deal around freedom needs clarifying, the following may help you.

First, look at how you're *defining* your offer: consider the four freedoms from earlier in this chapter. How would you describe what you're offering – or aspiring to offer, as it's usually work in progress – around autonomy, growth, self-expression and meaningful work?

Take a look at the more detailed definitions in Part 3, work your own collectively as a leadership team and test it with others to get valuable feedback.

Second, look at how you're *conveying* your offer:

Honesty: you're setting out a social (and legal) contract which you're inviting people to sign. Instead of seeking 1,000 solutions for 1,000 staff, it is more authentic to say, 'here's the deal so join us if you want to "play the game"'. I'm advocating clarity not ruthlessness, as clarity can be hugely motivating for people.

Reciprocity: freedom is a two-way street where both the organization and the individual are jointly responsible and with greater empowerment comes greater accountability. So, what are you asking people for in return?

Support: offering freedom without any structure or support is unfair as you won't be setting the team up for success. Make it clear how people will be supported while being held accountable for delivering their part.

Advice for individuals

What does freedom at work mean to you?

1. To explore this, set a timer for six minutes and answer the question by writing steadily without pausing until the

end.* If you prefer, try mind-mapping, voice-recording, or doodling your thoughts.

2. Re-read the short descriptions of the four freedoms above; which aspects of these resonate most strongly for you?
3. What else would you add into the mix that might be missing?
4. What do you value most about the freedom(s) you enjoy in your current role/with your present employer? What is this worth to you?
5. How do your age, race, gender, sexuality, ability or disability and other diversity traits play into your current experience of freedom at work – do these advantage or disadvantage you in any way?

Freedom's roots

In this chapter we've looked at what freedom at work means today, but how much do you know about where these freedoms came from? Understanding how past events and people have shaped the concept and practices of freedom at work over the centuries helps us to appreciate why things are the way they are today. It's interesting to recognize trends and to hazard a guess or two about where freedom might be headed in the future. So, in the next chapter I'll step back in time and chart freedom's progress over the years.

* This is a technique known as exploratory writing, introduced to me by my publisher Alison Jones. To discover more, I recommend her book *Exploratory Writing: everyday magic for life and work.*

Chapter 5
The freedom evolution

'I could not imagine that the future I was walking toward could compare in any way to the past that I was leaving behind.'

Nelson Mandela

Freedom, what freedom?

IF YOU'RE STUCK on Teams calls all day long, regularly working out-of-hours, been called back into the office five days a week, or if you dare not speak up honestly at work, then I can understand your scepticism. In our fast-evolving world of work, it's easy for forget that many of the work-related freedoms we enjoy today were fought for and won by others before us, often at great personal risk and even in return for life itself.

In this chapter, I'll chart some of the key people and events in history that have shaped workers' rights and support and led to the freedoms we benefit from now. In parallel, organizational theory and practices have evolved substantially over recent decades, changing the way work is managed and resourced and our lived experience of work. I'll also pinpoint how the Fourth Industrial Revolution – the rise of modern technology – has simultaneously expanded and limited our freedoms at work, what people aspire to today and what tomorrow heralds. For leaders there's advice on anticipating and responding to future workplace freedoms and for individuals, an invitation to reflect on your personal work freedoms, past, present and future.

Freedom fighters

Among the earliest known activists for workers' rights was an individual who lived not far from where I live today. In 1381, Wat Tyler, a labourer from Kent, England, led a peasants' uprising against King Richard II arguing for economic and social reform and was murdered for his efforts. Several centuries later, the Tolpuddle Martyrs – six agricultural labourers from the village of Tolpuddle in Dorset – were convicted in 1834 for the crime of self-organizing a peaceful response to harsh wage cuts heralding starvation. Transported to Australia, they were later pardoned and most of them emigrated to Canada.

A year after the Martyrs trial, in Philadelphia, the General Strike in 1835 by 20,000 workers calling for the ten-hour workday successfully gained them this right. A couple of decades later, Australia led the world in enshrining in law, in 1856, the eight-hour workday thanks to protesting skilled stonemasons, whose slogan of 'eight hours' work, eight hours' rest and eight hours' recreation' is commemorated by the 888 statue in Melbourne.

Not all campaigns ended successfully or without bloodshed; in the Haymarket Affair in Chicago in 1886, a peaceful strike by factory workers calling for the eight-hour workday ended in violence with police and deaths on both sides. Four years later, carpenters in the same city were the first group to win this right.

The battle for workers' freedoms wasn't just about hours and pay but welfare too and increasingly during the 20th century, focused on women. The 'Uprising of the 20,000' in New York in 1909 where mainly female Jewish garment workers protested against exploitation, sexual harassment, and dangerous conditions, ended one year before the tragedy of the Triangle Shirtwaist Factory in Manhattan where 146 workers – predominantly women and girls – died in a fire. While women's greater participation in the labour force during the two World Wars was subsequently suppressed, it did lead to longer-term advances in women's rights and equality at work. One landmark protest in the UK was by the Ford sewing machinists strike in 1968 where a group of women machinists employed at Ford's Dagenham plant (in Essex) demanded equal pay for equal work; they were ultimately successful and their action played a significant part in the later passing of equal pay legislation.

A slow path to freedom

The above are a few highlights from a much fuller story. But the courage and determination of these freedom fighters ultimately contributed to the effecting of the following UK legislation:

1906 and 1911: the introduction of the State pension and National Insurance protections respectively.

1963: the Contracts of Employment Act gave workers the right to written employment terms.

1965: the Race Relations Act made it illegal for individuals to experience discrimination as a result of their race.

1970: the Equal Pay Act was passed and came into force five years later; it required employers to pay women the same rate as men for equivalent work.

1975: the Sex Discrimination Act similarly protected women from gender-based inequalities.

1998: the Working Time Regulations safeguarded workers' entitlement to paid holidays and work breaks.

1998: the National Minimum Wage was established, upgraded to the National Living Wage in 2016.

2003: the repeal of Section 28 improved LGBTQ+ rights generally.

2010: the Equality Act defined 'protected characteristics' at work such as race, sex, disability, religion and age.

2015: the Modern Slavery Act aimed to reduce human trafficking and slavery.

Key milestones in the US include:

1829: the first formal union of workers was recognized.

1865: the abolition of slavery.

1866: the National Labor Union was founded.

1912: the first Department of Labor was established, with the first Secretary of Labor appointed the following year.

1938: the Fair Labor Standards Act introduced a federal minimum wage.

1963: women gained equal pay rights to men (earlier than in the UK).

1970: the Occupational Health and Safety Act mandated improvements in working conditions.

2020: while the murder of George Floyd sparked widespread diversity and inclusion initiatives in many organizations, at the time of writing it has not resulted in new legislation protecting black workers.

With regard to paid time off, current legislation varies significantly around the world:[†]

- In the European Union, from 2003 EU member states were required to offer at least four weeks paid annual leave per year; many countries offer more.

† A full list of minimum annual leave by country can be found on Wikipedia.

- In China, the statutory minimum is five days, more for tenure exceeding ten years.
- In the US, there is famously no federal right to paid time off; 77% of private employers offer some, averaging 10 days per year.

Systems, servants, and sweet spots

In parallel with the advancement of workers' rights, management practices have similarly evolved over the decades, impacting the amount and nature of freedom people have experienced in their work lives.

One strand of management thinking has sought to tightly define and control work steps and people's contributions. Scientific management, developed by Frederick Taylor in the early 20th century, favoured the systematic analysis of work processes and the belief that ignorant workers were there to obediently pump out widgets, not identify how to do things better – that role was reserved exclusively for managers. Profitability went up, workers' freedom did not. The Lean Principles for continuous improvement of the 1950s and the data-driven Six Sigma methodology of the 1990s similarly focused on streamlining processes, reducing errors and waste, and improving efficiency and quality.

Another strand, emerging in the 1960s, spotted that the richness of human potential was being overlooked. In contrast to traditional Theory X thinking that asserted people were unwilling to put in effort and should be tightly supervised (today's disparaging phrase 'shirking from home' being a modern example), Theory Y recognized that people are naturally self-motivated and with the right support, will willingly apply themselves in creative ways. Later on, Theory Z took this further, promoting a strong, cohesive culture, and greater emphasis on employee performance over hours worked. The concept of servant leadership argued that leaders should coax the best out of their employees by prioritizing their needs and demonstrating empathy.

With the rise of the global, networked organization, it became impossible to precisely monitor every employee's activity, so how best to co-ordinate effectively? Professor Robin Dunbar, an evolutionary psychologist, advises organizing around 'Dunbar's number', this being 'the size of group where things work most efficiently. If you have a group that's too small or too large, somehow it just falls apart. There's a sweet spot, which turns out to be at about 150 [people]'.[1] More radical thinkers and leaders have advocated, for example in the manifesto *Unboss*, for a holacracy whereby self-organizing groups replace hierarchy and established processes and decision-making is distributed across the organization instead of being concentrated at the top. Is this a recipe for the ultimate work freedom or chaos?

The impact of technology

Probably the single biggest impact on people's work freedom has been the advancement of technology. Thirty years ago, my father's law firm relied on analogue landlines, typewriters, and employees who lived within a half-hour drive of the office. Today's digital nomads WFA (work from anywhere) and fully distributed companies[‡] such as Atlassian are successfully harnessing a diverse, globally dispersed, time-flexible workforce, all thanks to cutting-edge networking, communication, and collaboration technologies.

The breakneck developments in artificial intelligence (AI) capabilities and applications have been transforming many professionals' experiences of work for a while now. Eight in ten workers believe AI will impact their jobs with a roughly even split between the optimists (typically younger) and the pessimists (typically older).[2] For many this is a chance to reduce the grind and focus on more satisfying work: many younger workers use AI tools to locate information, answer emails, write documents, and solve problems.

[‡] Where all employees work remotely with no central office or HQ.

The meteoric rise in online meetings began with the enforced mass-remote working of the COVID-19 pandemic and has barely abated since. There's wide variation in how people feel about virtual meetings; interestingly what seems to matter most is the amount of freedom we have to control the experience, particularly the webcam.[3] The latest technology for virtual meetings includes intelligent cameras, recognition of non-verbal gestures, analysis of conversational tone, and even AI-led coaching of presenters. Whether celebrated or reviled, endless calls – and messaging – have resulted in a genuine conundrum about how to free up people's time and attention to do quality work. Organizations are experimenting with office design and layout and meeting-free hours and days; amusingly many are reverting to off-site, device-free workshops, walkshops,¶ and awaydays to coax the best thinking out of their team.

Less cheerfully, new forms of employee monitoring have also proliferated with common examples including the tracking of keystrokes, browser activity, application usage, and meeting participation. More sophisticated methods analyse biometric data such our facial expressions and body movements. French data watchdog CNIL fined Amazon in early 2024 for excessive and at times illegal employee surveillance. If you think you've gained freedom with the right to work from home, check the small print.

COVID-19's legacy

The pandemic stamped an indelible mark on many people's work lives. Leaders everywhere scrambled to implement new tools and ways of working at breakneck speed in order to keep connecting employees and serving clients. One chief executive told me they achieved three years of transformation in one month. In addition, our home lives and our health were broadcast directly to our bosses and colleagues as one HR Director reflected poignantly 'we can't unsee what we saw during COVID'.

¶ Where participants collaborate while walking, often in nature.

Post-pandemic, the negotiating table looks different. Work and career flexibility is a deal-breaker with people refusing to relinquish the autonomy gained during lockdowns. They're less prepared to put up with inadequately skilled managers who lack emotional intelligence or fail to deliver on their promises. They're less concerned about conforming to social and professional norms, whether these are about workwear or slowly grafting their way up the ladder, and they're more vocal about their employer's stance on broader political and social issues.

There are downsides though to our post-COVID-19 freedoms. It's more of a challenge to build a sense of community at work when people are in and out on different days. Work starts feeling more transactional and less relational, and we're more likely to feel disconnected from one another. While intra-team glue is often reasonably good, inter-team glue is often brittle and efforts to bring everyone together can feel uncomfortably like socializing with strangers. The disadvantages are experienced unequally; for example, younger people feel less engaged and less mentored when older workers aren't in, with reduced opportunity for learning from these more experienced colleagues, networking informally, and getting on senior managers' radar. Another characteristic of the post-COVID-19 workplace is the difficulty in persuading people to support office-wide initiatives or volunteer for one-off tasks: 'it's harder to help people give a damn' lamented one CEO to me.

Freedom today

Broadly, people today desire the right to work flexibly, with competitive pay and benefits, a culture that respects personal time, and opportunities to grow and develop. We want autonomy to shape our work lives in a way that suits us, whether for caring reasons, to do life admin, or to pursue specific interests. We expect to pursue a side hustle or a portfolio career, to take extended career breaks, to rapidly expand our skills, and to have squiggly, non-linear careers. We value fairness, openness, and acceptance of difference too, but these are second-order priorities.

These broad aspirations are fairly universal, with some cultural and generational nuances. In the US, people place greater value on being associated with success (the glow of business awards and achievements) and failure (the battle scars of unsuccessful ventures and challenging experiences). In the UK and Europe, we typically prioritize cultural fit, work environment, and social connections more. In Turkey, people attach greater weight to maintaining kinship ties at work whereas in India it's community networks and social support.[4]

Life-stage wise, there are striking attitudinal differences between early-, mid-, and late-stage career cohorts.[§] Gen X value work-life balance and autonomy and are more likely to stick with the status quo despite niggles; Gen Y priorities personalized learning opportunities, authenticity, and transparency, while Gen Z are tech-savvy and crave flexibility, financial stability, and social rewards such as praise and recognition.[5]

There's also a generational divide around career mobility and 'a job for life' versus 'a job for now'. Switching employers every two years is considered perfectly acceptable to Millennials who are hungry to advance. Some CEOs are more sceptical of these demands, observing that Gen Z are simply more vocal than preceding generations; despite their calls for faster progression a lot of them end up in exactly the same places at similar times in their careers to older workers.

Finally, our choice of role, company, or industry is likely influenced by the importance we personally attach to certain work freedoms: if you're working in retail, hospitality, or manufacturing, for example, you are probably more willing to compromise on work location flexibility but in return you might expect greater flexibility in shift scheduling, decent overtime pay, and attractive on-site benefits. Employers whose workforces are split between office- and place-based roles are having to get

[§] Baby Boomers were born between 1946–1964, Generation X between 1965–1980, Millennials/Gen Y between 1981–1996, and Gen Z between 1997–2012. Gen Alpha were born after 2012.

creative at offering different flavours of freedom to avoid per-
ceptions and complaints of unfairness.

Freedom tomorrow

What will work-related freedom look like in the years ahead?
A few clues hint at this. We know that our choice of jobs will look
different, with AI set to replace a quarter of work tasks in the US
and Europe.[6] Half of young workers believe AI will consume a
large portion of their job, versus a smaller proportion of workers
aged over 55.

It's likely many knowledge-economy workers (by which I mean
whose work involves the creation, use, and distribution of
knowledge and information rather than tangible, physical goods
and assets) will continue to enjoy time and location flexibility,
with the share of UK workers working remotely part-time having
remained steady for the past two years and the majority of US
employers offering structured hybrid-working arrangements.

We *might* regain more of our leisure time: numerous European
countries have already introduced legal rights for employees to
switch off or disconnect digitally out-of-hours, with a statutory
code of practice expected in the UK. Latin American countries
are reducing the maximum weekly working hours, and Spain is
due to pass a bill in late 2025 reducing weekly working hours from
40 to 37.5. Singapore will allow employees to convert unused
sick leave allowance into paid annual leave, while in Saudi Arabia
people will be able to swap overtime pay for leave too.

Our employers might be up for trialling new creative working
arrangements, thanks to large-scale, cross-sector, evaluated trials
such as in the UK, and talent-wise we'll find it easier to move roles
internally with the rise of tech-enabled talent marketplaces that
provide greater visibility of company-wide opportunities.

We might all finally enjoy the same freedoms, as other new
legislation encourages the continued dismantling of the race,

class, age, and other barriers that limit opportunities available to certain employee groups. The draft Equality (Race and Disability) Bill in the UK is proposing mandatory ethnicity and disability pay gap reporting and several countries including the UK, the US, and Singapore have been tightening up employers' responsibilities to prevent sexual harassment.

These are tentative predictions; the world of work is still in flux and today's wide variation in approaches will continue until there are some definitive longitudinal studies proving what works and some clear corporate winners and losers.

Advice for leaders

In the game *Exploding Kittens*, one lucky card allows players to 'look into the future' by sneaking a peek at the next three cards in the deck while another card permits them to covertly shuffle those top three cards around. Sadly, leaders don't enjoy such options in the world of work, but you can still be ready for the next chapter in freedom's evolution by:

1. *Prioritizing time away from the detail to horizon scan.* As a senior leader, your role is to see the bigger picture; you benefit from having more time out to ponder and reflect so free up more space in your diary for this than you feel comfortable with.
2. *Responding to the trends your way.* When it comes to the triangle of pay, flexibility, and interesting work from Chapter 2, decide which angle(s) you want to lead on. If you offer all three, be true to what you're trying to create – don't try to be all things to all people.
3. *Focusing on fairness rather than homogeneity.* As the CEO of a consulting business reflected to me: 'the reality is that people do look at the world of work differently today. There's a much more complex relationship with what keeps people in play'.

4. *Accepting that this global movement towards personalization will continue.* Increase the tailoring of work packages, career paths, and development programmes for different groups and individuals.

5. *Expecting the unpredictable and being prepared to respond swiftly.* As with Lorenz' butterfly effect, one single event somewhere else in our complex world can potentially have a massive impact on your organization's stance and course.

Advice for individuals

Whether you are setting out in your career, have been in work for a decade or two, or are seeing your current role as your last, you can gain some potentially valuable insights by reflecting on how freedom has evolved for you at work. Take a few minutes to consider these questions:

1. What freedoms have you experienced during your career? Try charting these along a timeline and see what you notice.

2. What has been the impact of this freedom – and any lack of freedom – on your performance at work, your wellbeing, and your career satisfaction?

3. What freedom(s) have *you* had to fight for and what strategies worked best?

4. Looking ahead, what freedoms feel most important to you over the next few years? Why?

5. How might you seek out or negotiate ways to realize these?

An organizational tug of war

Newton's Third Law of Motion states that for every action, there is an equal and opposite reaction and this applies to retention and work freedom too. For every positive initiative or generous benefit you and your organization implement to support your employees and encourage them to stay, there are equally powerful opposing forces pulling them away, as you'll discover in the next chapter.

Chapter 6
Anti-freedom forces

'Freedom and constraint are two aspects of the same necessity, which is to be what one is and no other.'
Attributed to Antoine de Saint-Exupéry

Headwinds and hindrances

IF IT WAS simply a matter of will, creating People Glue would be a whole load easier. But even the most enlightened and open-minded leaders face multiple sources of pressure that hinder their efforts to harness work-related freedom for the mutual benefit of their business and their employees. To advance successfully, they have to overcome or circumvent these constraints.

In this chapter, I'll examine the external forces that act as a drag on your efforts, from government and economic policies, geopolitical tensions, corporate financing models to the global trust crisis. I'll also identify some of the internal forces that exist within an organization such as our love-in with quick fixes, organizing models, cultural encumbrances, attitudes to risk, discomfort with change, and the reduction in social connectivity at work. At the end of the chapter there's a diagnostic to help you identify what's holding you back from offering more freedom in your organization and advice for anyone feeling held back at work by forces beyond their control.

If, as you read this chapter, you are acutely aware that you're facing a number of the challenges I describe, then you may be looking for reassurance that you can still find and hold onto good people in the global market and impatient to hear how best to achieve this. Let me state definitively upfront that yes, there are positive, practical steps you can take in your business to set out a compelling deal for employees and to give them a rewarding experience of work that inspires a deep loyalty over the longer-term. Part 3 helps you understand better what people want and need, and Part 4 sets out how you can respond to this – in a way that works for your business – through your organization design and ways of working, through your leadership approach, and through growing skilled people managers.

External forces

We before you

The globalization of work, including access to overseas talent, international collaborations, and the free movement of workers, has faced some challenges in recent years. This is partly due to the rise of nationalist and protectionist policies in both Western democracies and other nation states, where domestic industries are being prioritized over foreign investment, higher tariffs imposed on imports, increased scrutiny and transparency required around the offshoring of work, and tighter restrictions placed on immigration and the availability of work visas. Both the UK and US governments are taking measures to reduce international recruitment by tightening visa regulations and immigration criteria for overseas workers. These interventions directly impact businesses' ability to bring in the skills they need and to expand business operations overseas, and while today's worker might cherish the idea of working from anywhere (WFA), would-be digital nomads (and healthcare workers, teachers and other skilled professionals), are discovering that thanks to WFA taxation rules, the reality is not so simple.

Turf and trade wars

Another factor making it harder for businesses to operate freely, grow in new markets and recruit from a global talent pool is the rise in geopolitical tensions in various regions. These hostilities and wars bring additional complexities for leaders to resolve, such as sanctions restricting the flow of capital, goods and services, and onerous legal checks which add to employees' workloads. Supply chain costs can rise significantly when normal distribution routes are disrupted and the availability of valuable components is reduced. Barriers and uncertainty relating to international trade increased following Trump's trade wars. All of these consequences dent investor confidence and can cause investment levels, employment levels, and stock prices to dip; estimates suggest European companies have lost up to $100 billion in value as a result of Russia's invasion of Ukraine.[1]

Investor impatience

A third constraint acting on leaders and businesses is the short-term focus often favoured by investors hungry to realize their rewards and move on to the next opportunity. This is less of an issue for privately owned firms such as limited partnerships and more prevalent for executives at publicly listed companies and private equity-funded businesses. The former have greater freedom to do what they want, whether that means moving their margin around according to circumstance and/or proposing new working patterns that feel right for their business. The latter are more restricted because they've got shareholders and analysts to bring on side, or at least not put offside. Leaders can find this frustrating, particularly if they've been hired to grow the business but discover everything is about cost and margins.

As business school professor and author Cal Newport emphasizes in his brilliant book, *Slow Productivity*, producing great work takes time, but a very heavy focus on short-term goals and KPIs (key performance indicators) can overshadow the need for longer-term strategic thinking.

Mistrust

For 25 years, The Edelman Trust Institute has measured levels of trust in public institutions, the media, and leaders via its 'trust barometer', a global annual survey of over 33,000 individuals around the world. In all bar three countries, trust in employers has declined over the past year and barely moved since 2018. A staggering 68% of employees believe that their leaders have knowingly misled them with falsehoods or gross exaggerations, while a similar proportion hold grievances against the government, the wealthy, and businesses.

This societal crisis of trust plays out in different ways in the world of work, a salient example being the 'return to office' (RTO) power battle between employer and employee that arose post-COVID-19 and as yet shows little sign of abating. A corporate edict saying, 'we want you back five days a week' smacks of mistrust and a return to traditional 'management by walking around'. A leader loudly opining that working from home 'is not proper work' incenses workers who say they are at their most productive at home and ignores rigorous data confirming that two days a week remote working is as productive as five days a week in the office. Plus, as many a worker knows, people can be in the office and still not performing.

Internal forces

Magic wands and silver bullets

Faced with a shifting, complex business landscape, our innate desire to create structure and clarity out of chaos is understandable. We instinctively look for policies and methodologies that promise fast and certain relief and absolve us from the greater effort and persistence required to realize a deeper, more systemic solution. Witness our cult of the winning leadership model or management framework: leadership books and leaders' autobiographies consistently rank among the top-selling non-fiction books.

The problem is, these magic wands or silver bullets don't exist, however much the media persuades us otherwise. While levers such as the four-day week, job-sharing, or scrum methodology (a more agile way of managing projects than traditional approaches) can yield operational improvements, they're never going to be the answer to everything.

The silver bullet appeals because it lessens our anxiety, explains Steve Hearsum, author of *No Silver Bullet*. We either love it because we're relieved to have 'found' an organizational painkiller that will make our headache go away or because we can redirect any blame on to it if it doesn't work. A few years ago, at the global pharmaceutical giant Novartis, the new CEO wanted to foster a more empowered culture in order to strengthen their pipeline of innovative drugs. Leaders started talking about an 'inspired, curious, and unbossed' culture but the term 'unbossed' proved so seductive that employees and the media latched on to it and ran away with it. Ultimately, this approach to changing their culture backfired: so much talk about unbossing raised impossibly high expectations, when in reality it takes energy and time to achieve a shift in mindset and behaviour.

Organizing models

Another internal force acting against freedom is the design of the organization itself, i.e. its structures and processes. Often these can be a limiting factor when it comes to innovation because they frequently stifle creativity. Entrenched hierarchies can also cause deafness in the boardroom, where board members fail to tune in to operational realities and sufficiently explore all the possibilities; in regulated industries this may mean they don't constructively challenge regulatory proposals that could unnecessarily constrain the business' freedom to operate a certain way.

These constraints manifest not just in larger businesses but in smaller organizations too, particularly at key growth milestones. The people who helped the organization to grow in its early years may not be the right people needed as the business matures, for example, if there's a strategic shift from being R&D-led to becoming a commercial organization. Plus, the founder/CEO may have hired them personally but as the company grows, their direct access to that CEO reduces. These developments limit people's career options internally and also their freedom to operate.

The way people are organized – roles, job titles, skill groups – can unintentionally make people feel boxed in. Employers' focus on skills often reduces individuals to feeling labelled as X or Y skill instead of being appreciated for who they are as a person and all that they can bring. To counter this, think carefully about the person's potential and what they can contribute more broadly to the organization over the longer term.

Hamster wheels

In my first book, *The Future of Time*, I describe how extreme busyness and 'work about work' are examples of our unhealthy, unproductive cultural norms around how we spend our working hours. Speed and urgency dominate, so too does our collective tendency to add – new projects, new procedures, new responsibilities –– rather than subtract. We race ever faster on our hamster wheels and the more we have on our minds, the more we default to adding. In *The Friction Project*, Bob Sutton and Huggy Rao describe this 'addition sickness' as a source of destructive organizational friction, preventing people from delivering work with ease. Over the past two decades, the intensity of work has steadily increased[2] but much of this is what management expert and author John Kotter terms 'false urgency' or is simply going unnoticed: in one study, managers couldn't account for 60% of the work that colleagues were so busily delivering.[3]

Some of this extreme busyness is fuelled by the proliferation of virtual meetings and instant messaging in recent years. In just three years, the average number of Teams calls we participate in and the volume of chat messages we send have tripled. With 60% of these calls lasting less than 15 minutes, our time and attention are chopped into tiny fragments, our (effortful) cognitive switching increases and an astonishing chunk of our annual work time is lost to this 'toggling tax', reducing our freedom to get on with meaningful work.

For many, offices have become distraction factories and even when working remotely, people lack sufficient focus time; most of us don't get enough uninterrupted time during 'normal' working hours. This inability to focus has become one of the most pressing and knotty issues organizations are wrestling with and it is estimated to cost employers US$34,448 per person in lost productivity according to the Economist Intelligence Unit.

Fear of failure

Competence is valued so highly at work that we've cultivated a collective aversion to taking risks and failing. Promotion decisions typically favour a steady pair of hands who's unlikely to drop the ball and weed out risk takers. People's desire or ability to propose new ideas can be inhibited; if you're leading an organization or department and you're not visibly taking risks, trying new ideas, and celebrating failure then your team won't do it either. It boils down to basic psychology – how you as a leader interact with others signals whether it's ok to bring ideas and concerns forward or not. A common fear I hear leaders articulate is of the consequences of failing to meet everyone's needs or expectations equitably. You may genuinely be trying to find a balance that works for your business *and* your employees but end up hamstrung by perceived unfairness because as people typically value different things, some may end up feeling disadvantaged or excluded. While there may not be a perfect answer that makes everyone happy, if people have the opportunity to raise their concerns directly and have an open conversation, they tend to content to compromise simply because they have felt heard and acknowledged.

Comfort over change

While greater freedom sounds enticing, it's human nature for all of us to favour the status quo. In organizations we're typically conditioned to want direction, escalate up decisions, and seek approval; for some, freedom can feel particularly daunting and they may flourish better in a more tightly controlled environment.

Change and ambiguity are by their nature uncomfortable, forcing us to let go of things we may value deeply such as aspects of our professional identity, competence, or trusted relationships. It's tempting to hang on to comfortable work because it's less effortful and less risky than branching out. But attitudes such as 'we've always done it like this and we've always been successful' lead to blind spots and missed opportunities. When we get curious and stick our heads up above the parapet to see what others are doing – whether colleagues, clients, or competitors – we get inspired and spot potential collaborations. But this takes courage and contrary to what we might think courage isn't innate but a skill we all have to practice. Through regular, everyday practice we can reduce our fear level and get more comfortable with discomfort.

Reduced connectivity

We may be digitally connected like never before, but as Noreena Hertz describes in her powerful book *The Lonely Century*, it has become easier to avoid day-to-day contact with others thanks to online shopping, messaging, and the digitalization of services. Against the backdrop of neoliberalism, we have become 'competitors not collaborators, consumers not citizens, hoarders not sharers, takers not givers, hustlers not helpers', making it harder to bring people together and connect meaningfully. For leaders there's a difficult tension between balancing people's desire to work autonomously and remotely with cultivating an enriching sense of community: giving people complete freedom to work how they want, when they want, can come at the cost of company culture and cohesion.

Natural groupings at work may remain resilient, but achieving connectivity across those groups is far harder. Cross-functional collaboration brings different perspectives into play that can spark creativity, so that the problem being explored becomes clearer with those different insights and the solutions being generated become richer. Many companies struggle with being too siloed, but if you can address this successfully, then people understand better the fuller picture of your business and can talk more knowledgeably to clients about this.

From a retention perspective, when the quality and quantity of our social bonds at work reduces, with fewer shared in-person experiences, spontaneous exchanges, and face-to-face informal mentoring, in parallel our relationship with our employer becomes more transactional too, creating a looser tie and ultimately making it easier to walk away. Cognizant of this, some organizations are successfully bringing people together in more intentional ways at regular intervals, both to work and to have fun together.

Advice for leaders

What's holding you back from offering more freedom? Invite your executive or management team to reflect on the anti-freedom forces detailed above and how they may be constraining your business. These same forces are summarized in the table below; rank the forces that are having the greatest impact on your business at the top and those impacting you the least at the bottom, or group them into 'high', 'medium', and 'low'. Add other forces that you've observed too.

Anti-freedom forces	Impact on our business
Lack of sector-wide collaboration	
Local legislation and regulation	
Restrictions on our access to international talent and/or talent mobility	
Geopolitical tensions and supply chain disruptions	
Short-term business pressures and insufficient long-term focus	
Trust in leaders	
Preference for silver bullets and quick fixes	
Organizational model (structures, processes and mindsets)	
Extreme busyness, distractions and lack of focus time	
Fear of failure	
Preference for the status quo and/ or lack of curiosity	
Insufficient inter-team connectivity	

What could you do differently about the forces that are hindering you the most? How can you learn from newer players in the market or from other sectors? How could you crowdsource ideas from employees for overcoming or circumventing these constraints?

Advice for individuals

Here are three resources that can help you strengthen your own agency in the face of social, organizational, or internal (e.g., mindset) forces that may be limiting your freedom in your own work life.

1. *Intellectual humility quiz.* Developed by the Greater Good Science Center at the University of California, Berkeley, this assessment helps you to recognize the limitations of your own knowledge and beliefs and encourage greater curiosity. You can take the quiz here: https://greatergood. berkeley.edu/quizzes/take_quiz/intellectual_humility

2. *Stephen Covey's Circles of Influence and Concern.* Drawn from his book, *The 7 habits of highly effective people*, this model is formed of two concentric circles where the outer Circle of Concern represents everything we worry about and the inner Circle of Influence represents those things over which we have some control or influence. By focusing on the latter, we can strengthen our own resourcefulness and invest our energy effectively.

3. *Bonding versus bridging social capital.* This social networks concept was introduced by sociologist Mark Granovetter and expanded by political scientist Robert Putnam. *Bonding* social capital refers to our connections *within* familiar groups; this acts as glue to build strong cohesive teams and enable the smooth execution of plans and strategies. *Bridging* social capital refers to our connections *across* groups; this brings us diverse insights with innovative or transformative potential. In a changing context, maintaining both sets of connections can help us spot developments early and respond to them effectively.

The quest continues

In Part 2, we've seen how work-related freedom is not a static or fixed concept but a moving point on a continuum that stretches far back into our social history and is extending forward daily into our near and distant future. It's not a straight line but an uneven one, with bumps and bends as major developments shape work legislation, policies and practices, and external and internal forces impact our intentions. Following on from Part 2's initial introduction to what freedom at work is, in Part 3 I'll dive deeper into each of the four freedoms and explain how they individually and collectively contribute to creating a 'sticky' work culture that persuades people to stay.

Part 3
The four freedoms

'I am no bird, and no net ensnares me: I am a free human being with an independent will.'

Charlotte Brontë

Chapter 7
Autonomy

'Man is ultimately self-determining. What he becomes – within the limits of endowment and environment – he has made out of himself.'
Victor Frankl

Honing in

THIS CHAPTER, AND the following three, analyse the four freedoms – autonomy, growth, self-expression, and meaningful work – in turn from both the individual employee's and the employer's perspectives. I'll set out how important each freedom is to people and why; draw out some of the nuances around each freedom; identify the consequences of high and low levels of each freedom; and look at how to balance individuals' needs and preferences with business needs and realities. Part 4 guides you through successfully implementing these freedoms in your organization.

To recap, this first freedom of autonomy encompasses flexibility, control, and the freedom not to work at times. This is about when, where, and how people work and the extent to which they can structure their working day and week as they see fit. It's about influencing decisions relating to their own work, improving ways of working, and being trusted to deliver. Finally, it's about being able to switch off from work without being pressured to be available out-of-hours.

Today's dealbreaker

Make no mistake, autonomy matters. Flexibility and work-life balance are today as important and/or more important to people as pay;[1] more than 75% of us would decline job offers that negatively impact our home lives;[2] and people who feel micromanaged are particularly likely to consider changing jobs.

Giving people autonomy recognizes that we all work in different ways and are at our most productive at different times and in different settings; also, that our motivations and needs vary at each stage of life. We all need to feel – to a greater or lesser extent – that we have some agency over our work lives. HiPos (high potential employees) especially thrive on autonomy and expect to progress quickly or just as swiftly, or they'll leave to gain this elsewhere. Anecdotally in conversations about freedom at work, most people I speak to instinctively tend to think first of autonomy and flexibility and in my survey sample, respondents were almost universally agreed on the *importance* of autonomy. There were subtle nuances though across age groups, gender, and current working arrangement as the table below shows.

Freedom	Valued most by	Valued less by
Autonomy	Leaders and managers; remote- and hybrid-workers; older employees; men.	Younger employees; women (who rated this only slightly lower than men); office-based workers.

Here's why autonomy matters to some respondents:

> Autonomy in all aspects of my career – where I work, how I work, who I work for – is what essentially fulfils me and makes me happy.

> It has been crucial to my ability to remain in the workplace and continue a career while also looking after a young family.

> The worst feeling you can have in a job is waking up and dreading work, but feeling unable to leave or unable to change anything.

People recognize that autonomy matters so much partly because it is a relatively recent, hard-won freedom post-COVID-19. They're also wary of greedy employers and ridiculous workloads, where autonomy becomes meaningless and 'just a way to extract more from you at work and at home'.

When ranking their *experiences* of autonomy, a striking difference emerged between genders and between leaders and non-leaders, as shown in the table below.

Freedom	Experienced most by	Experienced less by
Autonomy	Women; employees aged 45+ (excluding leaders); white British/ European employees.	Men; employees aged under 35; leaders; Asian, Black and mixed-race employees.

With regard to the gender variation, this may be due to proportionally more women working in part-time, job-share, and other flexible roles because they've traditionally been the primary carer. This factor may also play into the leader/non-leader variation: fewer women occupy leadership roles in the UK (and other countries) and both male and female leaders tended to report lower autonomy due to their heavy workloads and expectation to be constantly available. While you might have more control in senior positions over *how you do* your work, the demands of leadership likely reduce your work life balance and freedom *from* work.

Autonomy over *where* you work

Freedom to choose your location of work has probably been the most-debated aspect of autonomy of late but despite attention-grabbing headlines amplifying the more extreme decisions, location flexibility has settled into a fairly steady pattern in the UK as shown in Figure 3, with hybrid-working being the most common model. The picture in the US is broadly similar.[3]

This is undoubtedly in response to employee demand and people's unwillingness to relinquish location flexibility post-pandemic: 75% say that ability to work flexibility and from wherever they want is critical.[4] While working from home twice a week has no proven impact on employee or business performance, it does reduce

Figure 3 How work models have stabilized

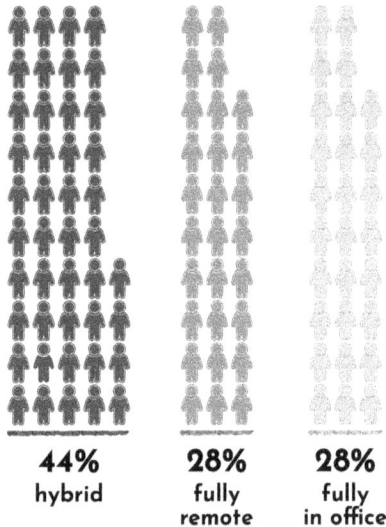

| 44% | 28% | 28% |
| hybrid | fully remote | fully in office |

employee turnover by a third, saving employers significant costs.[5] Following hybrid-working trials, managers shifted from being productivity sceptics to net positive. Here's one professional's perspective:

> Working from home when I need to is a game-changer. I love the office environment and miss it when I can't get in but I'm also super-productive when I work from home. Hybrid all the way for me!

Less fortunate employees whose employers insist they return to the office five days a week are more likely to quit; research into this trend shows that turnover rates are highest for female employees and more skilled colleagues, and vacancies in those organizations remain unfilled for longer compared to organizations without RTO mandates. As one individual shared with me:

> Lack of freedom to decide where to work in my previous role ultimately led to me quitting. It was not the only factor, but a key one. I increasingly felt I no longer had the freedom to choose how to do my job well.

Autonomy over *when* you work

Since the pandemic, informal day-to-day time flexibility has become more accepted and transparent. In office-based work, popping out to do an errand or pick up a child no longer raises eyebrows while in place-based work there's been a corresponding rise in self-rostering and shift-swapping (the ability to choose your shifts and swap them with colleagues). In contrast, levels of formal (i.e., contractual) part-time working, including job-sharing, remain broadly unchanged and access to this is unequal. Many people are stuck in low quality, low paid work because they want to work part-time; meanwhile in higher-paid sectors and roles, people who are trying to make their careers work part-time still encounter substantial attitudinal and progression barriers.

What does time-related autonomy mean to people? In their words: 'the ability to be flexible when family or other demands dictate'; 'being trusted to manage my life and work in balance, including flexing my work hours on a day-to-day basis'; 'being able to come in later or leave earlier to avoid being trapped in clogged public transport'. Time flexibility is highly valued because people's home life pressures vary at different points in the year and from year to year plus attitudes have changed. What people want is the freedom for work not to be the 'be all and end all' of their lives; a study of 10,000 workers across six countries confirmed those experiencing burnout were over three times more likely to look for a job elsewhere.[6]

Businesses that see time flexibility's potential as a win-win benefit trial initiatives such as advertising all roles as flexible and offering greater leave flexibility, track relevant metrics, and take evidence-based decisions. They're also deploying increasingly sophisticated tools such as AI-based intelligent resourcing and rostering to better respond to business peaks while accommodating individual employees' preferences.

Autonomy over *how* you work

This is about freedom to operate: people's ability to get on with their work as they choose, from managing their priorities, organizing their workload and collaborating with others, to trying out novel ideas and improving work processes:

Managing my own workload as I see fit.

Being able to decide how I get things done.

Determining my priorities when there are competing demands.

Deciding how I perform my tasks at work, in which order and when.

There are nuances: for younger workers the emphasis is on freedom to execute agreed tasks while for more experienced professionals the freedom to set the direction matters more:

> Having autonomy to set goals and prioritize, to speak to stakeholders without asking 'permission', to manage my own time and deadlines, to control the operational budget.

> I'm at a stage in my career where growth has less importance and the content of the daily tasks and how I'm able to execute them have more.

People loathe being excessively supervised or constrained by gatekeepers who limit their access to critical information or decision-makers. Freedom to operate means having the space to execute their work without others breathing down their neck or questioning every step:

> Being judged on output rather than micromanaged on process.

> Being fully trusted to do my job.

> Having the freedom to make my own decisions, not be micro-managed.

Setting up autonomy over how people work starts early as the European CEO of a global consumer products business observed to me:

> It's crucial to have a fully honest two-way conversation about mutual expectations before people join. If the interview process is simply a sales pitch on both sides, then in the first year the new joiner muscles on through and is engaged but the second year becomes a challenge.

So, during the interview process, openly explore what candidates need to make the role sustainable and enjoyable by asking questions like 'what gives you energy?' and 'what support do you need inside and outside of the company to make this work?'.

A no-brainer

Experiments by neuroscientists confirm that increased autonomy results in greater discretionary effort and productivity. But do these lab findings also hold true in the work environment?

One fascinating year-long trial involving 76 companies and 25,000 employees ascertained that when meetings were reduced by 40%, the outcomes shown in Figure 4 were identified.[7]

Productivity went up because employees felt more empowered and autonomous, and consequently they held themselves more accountable for their own performance. These trial results are anecdotally borne out by professionals I've interviewed:

> Generally being treated like an adult rather than surveilled has been especially positive.

> Autonomy is crucial to maintaining my good mental health.

> The organization's trust in letting me perform my tasks as I think best makes me more motivated and willing to share my experiences with colleagues.

Figure 4 The impact of two meeting-free days

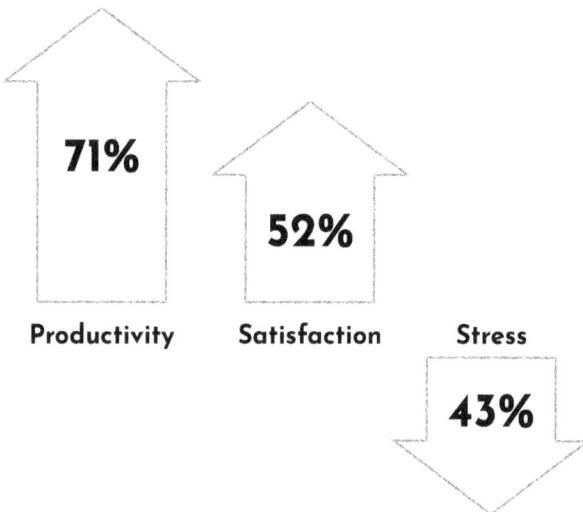

71%

52%

Productivity   Satisfaction   Stress

43%

Other benefits include advancing people's leadership skills and enhancing their subject-matter expertise, resulting in higher quality work. People feel they can bring their best skills and insights to their work thanks to the autonomy they enjoy:

> Autonomy has led to growth, allowed me to connect with new colleagues and in turn this has enhanced my productivity and outputs – so a real win for me and the business.

Analysis of over 450,000 ratings on the jobs site Glassdoor has identified that flexibility positively impacts employee sentiment towards their employer, with those organizations offering more flexibility receiving the highest ratings for company culture, values, and career advancement.

Autonomy reduces turnover and increases retention by enabling people to stay in their jobs for the longer-term:

> Greater autonomy as I've become more senior has kept my challenging career/role (just about) manageable despite the demands of it increasing year on year.

As an example, in a six month randomized control trial led by Stanford University Economic Professor Nick Bloom, when employees worked two days a week from home, job satisfaction rose and quit rates reduced by one third.[8] Finally, autonomy frees people up to be innovative and to generate game-changing possibilities:

> The more autonomy I have, the more room I have to be creative, which is fundamentally important if a business wants to stay fit for the future.

This is echoed in one leader's memorable observation that:

> Every organization is decaying from its core, the question is how fast you're innovating to overcome this rate of decay.

If you want your business to be around long into the future, offer autonomy.

Slow poison

The absence or denial of autonomy leads to damaging consequences for individuals and for their organizations. It erodes people's intrinsic motivation and has a lasting after-effect where people report reduced self-belief over the longer-term. Here's one professional's story:

> I was micromanaged in a job many years ago by an awful boss with no people skills. I left as soon as I found another role, but the experience affected my confidence and it was only thanks to the very competent and kind boss in the new role that I recovered quickly.

An environment of mistrust and micromanagement breeds the twin evils of pessimism and negativity. People have described to me how they became cynical and withdrawn, resentful of the hours they were putting in and miserable at work. When the confines of people's roles are drawn too tightly, their work content becomes tediously familiar, depressing people's positive outlook and job satisfaction. Their commitment goes down, the impetus to move grows:

> I see our freedoms and autonomy being gradually stripped away and it is making me question my ability and my reason for being there.

Time after time, people have told me that in such circumstances, they ended up leaving for greater autonomy and a more enjoyable role elsewhere. A poor work-life balance contributes to high turnover and lack of work flexibility influences people's decision to leave. Reducing location flexibility through RTO mandates correlates with lower performance, lower employee scores for work-life balance, job satisfaction, and senior leadership;[9] meanwhile even leaders themselves aren't immune to curbs on autonomy with a third of executives called back into the office by mandate saying they'd leave their employer as a result.[10]

Equilibrium

To offer autonomy successfully doesn't mean granting unfettered freedom; it does require some boundaries. Back to the parenting analogy: while teenagers test authority in their bid for independence, they're simultaneously reassured by lines in the sand which can't be crossed, even if they don't admit this. They gradually learn that it's only by sticking to the mutually agreed terms of engagement that they can enjoy their greater freedom. After all, those terms also secure them the support and (looser) structure they still want and need, from their favourite home-cooked meals to that emergency lift when the bus gets cancelled. There's a point of equilibrium which might occasionally wobble either way but while it's broadly being met, both parties can operate pretty autonomously.

Providing autonomy at work is similarly about creating the right structure and boundaries too, such as setting out transparently what you expect from people in their roles and what decision-making authority they have and clarifying tasks and priorities. On working pattern flexibility, leaders have to strike a careful balance between recognizing people's individual preferences, attending to the group dynamics and meeting the operational needs of the business. If you want to build a 'sticky' work culture founded on reciprocal relationships of trust and collaboration, then it's very hard to achieve that without people spending some time together. Even fully distributed firms like Atlassian still meet in-person, they're just very intentional about when and how. Work transactions run more smoothly and issues can be quickly resolved when the underlying relationships are strong.

People absolutely recognize this need for equilibrium: they want to get their work done in a timely way so as not to hold up colleagues awaiting their input. They understand that sometimes there's a vital need to follow a set process rather than go off-piste; they appreciate that co-ordination (and compromise) bring mutual benefits; and finally, they appreciate that their own decision-making powers should respect the scope of their role.

Advice for leaders

Take a fresh look at the autonomy you're offering to your employees and consider ways to increase this without relinquishing the critical boundaries. These five questions may help you:

1. *If you've recently changed (or are planning to change) any formal policies or informal practices, what's the impact?* Have you seen an uptick in vacancy applications, time to fill, or internal talent progression, particularly with care-givers? Or are higher numbers leaving for more flexible competitors or sectors, and who's going?

2. *Where's the energy?* Which teams are fizzing with creative ideas, rising to every challenge and knocking it out the park performance-wise? This suggests they're putting autonomy to good use.

3. *Where might the 'slow poison' effect (described above) be manifesting?* Look for teams with higher-than-average rates of attrition or applications to move sideways; any stubbornly low engagement survey scores; any under-performing employees previously identified as having potential.

4. *What's the picture across your managers?* Are they lightly managing the boundaries or applying rigidity? Do they lean towards autocratic or empowering? How does that compare to their team's effectiveness?

5. *How could you conduct your own trial?* Commission a team (existing or temporary) to resolve a business issue or explore an opportunity. Give them greater autonomy, ask them what support they need, and track key metrics.

Advice for individuals

Take a few minutes to reflect on the autonomy you desire or enjoy in your own work life.

1. *Use the Appreciative Inquiry technique* to leverage your autonomy at work to your (and your employer's) advantage.* Reflect on a time when you did your best work (define that as you wish). What role did autonomy play in this? What did it enable you to do? How can you apply any learnings to your work today?

2. *Explore opportunities in your present role to expand your autonomy.* Could you propose an experiment with your manager and agree together what success would look like? If you're frustrated by your manager's tendency to over-supervise, sometimes your differing needs for detail and visibility can be a factor. How could you communicate together differently in a way that better meets both your needs? e.g., a weekly email update or a regular 'heads up' conversation.

3. *Consider any future opportunities through the three autonomy lenses of 'what', 'when' and 'how'.* What do you value most right now and why? If you're thinking about an internal or external move, how can you open up a dialogue early in the process about your mutual expectations regarding autonomy?

---

* If you've not heard of this, a good overview is in this Positive Psychology article: https://positivepsychology.com/appreciative-inquiry/.

Purposeful progress

In this chapter we've seen how autonomy is about flexibility and agency, within appropriate organizational boundaries, as well as a means of achieving a sustainable equilibrium between our work and home lives. Let's turn now to look more closely at the second freedom – growth – and how this can help people to develop personally and professionally and advance in their careers, benefiting the businesses they work for too.

Chapter 8
Growth

'Lock up your libraries if you like; but there is no gate, no lock, no bolt, that you can set upon the freedom of my mind.'

Virginia Woolf

Cultivating careers

BACK IN CHAPTER 2, one of the golden triangle's three points related to 'interesting work'. This encompasses both the nature or content of people's work and their ability to extend their expertise through formal and informal development opportunities. We also saw how one of the common triggers for people choosing to leave is feeling stuck and overlooked in their career. In this chapter I'll unpack further what 'freedom to grow' means to people, what growth they're seeking and what they've experienced at work during their careers so far.

Not everyone has ambitions to advance: having reached a certain level of competence in a role they find satisfying, some are content to explore that experience to the full without chasing another promotion. All organizations need a certain number of these experienced, reliable colleagues whose 'safe hands' are vital for operational stability, service quality, and continuity. However, businesses also need to continuously upskill a big chunk of their workforces in order to have sufficient internal capability to meet future demand.

In this chapter, I'll explore why growth is a must-have for individuals and their employers alike; I'll look at the benefits of growth and what happens when people lack freedom to grow; and I'll touch on some creative ways in which innovative organizations are enabling professional growth. Finally, the end-of-chapter advice for leaders and individuals will help you look afresh at the growth pathways you're illuminating for others and for yourself.

Growth charts

Why does growth matter so much? After all, we've all been getting smarter with every passing generation according to the Flynn effect.*

Businesses can't afford to ignore the professional growth of their employees for multiple reasons. By 2030, demand for skilled workers will exceed supply, causing a global 'talent crunch' where employers will be short of 85 million sought-after individuals and US$8 trillion globally in unrealized revenue.[1] Additionally, as seen in earlier chapters, the jobs of the future will look very different to those of today, requiring skills that are still emergent; the World Economic Forum launched a Reskilling Revolution initiative to help economies adapt to the tech landscape of the future and to provide a billion people with future-ready skills to secure good quality job opportunities. Finally, a higher-skilled employee base enables businesses to respond better to disruption, shore up productivity levels, and reduce commercial vulnerability.

Clearly it's a strategic imperative, so businesses are making this their top priority, right? Well, yes and no. Employers *have* been

---

* The steady increase in IQ scores in countries around the world over the last century, documented by intelligence researcher James Flynn.

investing in learning, development, and career progression over recent years but this is a mixed picture with some concerning gaps. In the UK, overall employer investment in training per employee has declined since 2005 to just half of the EU average.[2]

Various sizeable studies point to people's increasing dissatisfaction with the support offered by their employer to grow their expertise, with many saying:

- They don't feel encouraged to learn new skills.
- Their manager doesn't talk to them about their growth.
- Their employer doesn't provide sufficient opportunity to gain career-enhancing skills.
- Their employer relies heavily on external hires.
- Their company is a 'talent magnet' (excels at hiring) and not a 'talent factory' (excels at developing).

Not everyone gets access to the same growth and advancement opportunities; this freedom is definitely not enjoyed by all because it's not a level playing field. Consequently women, people with disabilities, people of colour, and those from lower socio-economic backgrounds are significantly under-represented in manager roles and leadership tiers[3] and there is much more organizations can do to prepare people and tap into the rich talent they have, instead of always seeking experienced hires externally. With almost half of employees saying that the opportunity to grow their skills is a major factor in deciding whether to stay or leave, the lack of such opportunities for diverse employees is shortening their tenure and intensifying homogeneity at leadership levels.

Growth stories

People who've enjoyed freedom to grow have valued being in an environment where growth is not just limited to specific skills for their present role but about their broader psychological development too, and where feedback is openly and generously offered. They've worked for firms that take a flexible approach to employees' skillsets rather than slotting them into existing moulds, and they observe that this tends to happen in organizations that believe in you as a *person*, not just as a role holder. This chimes with how one leader reflected, in conversation with me, about how she is viewed: 'What am I in this organization? Am I an asset? Am I a talent? Above all for me it is important to be deeply human and valued and valuable'.

Growth is not just about skills but about relationships too, and having the freedom to associate with others like us and different to us through internal and external networking opportunities, membership associations, shared interest communities, and study groups. In *Working Identity*, Professor Herminia Ibarra of INSEAD business school shows how interacting in new social networks enables us to develop professionally and continuously evolve our expertise and our sense of self.

Less positively a very hierarchical organization, where each level has tightly defined boundaries for decision-making and responsibilities, stifles people as do rigid and narrow frameworks. 'With 20+ years of experience and knowledge in the area, it was demotivating to be labelled a junior simply because I lacked a specific qualification' lamented one professional in my research. Others have waited too long for promised opportunities to materialize, then exited feeling let down.

In his book *Range*, David Epstein explains how 'dancing across disciplines' enables us to think more creatively and solve problems more effectively. He shares the metaphor of an eight-lane highway where moving across different roles and specialisms, particularly early on in our careers, makes us more adaptable. People have reported to me their deep frustration with managers who want them to stay in their lane and prevent them from switching or widening their lane.

Sometimes the reverse is true and we need a nudge to step out of our familiar lane, even in senior roles. One global leader described to me a significant turning point for them:

I decided I needed to get comfortable with being very uncomfortable. The worst that can happen is that at first I don't do things to the best of my ability, but next time I will do. So I need to embrace it, learn from the experience and allow myself the opportunity to maybe fail a little bit.

Being in a culture where failure is encouraged and treated as a learning activity is highly prized – without freedom to fail, there's no freedom to grow.

Pots of gold

Top of people's wish lists when it comes to growth are (in order) to:

1. Make progress towards their career goals.

2. Keep updating their expertise.

3. Spend more time on learning.

4. Access personalized learning aligned to their interests and career aspirations.

When they're mulling over a move, three of their top five considerations are:

1. Challenging work.

2. Having opportunities internally to grow their career.

3. Learning and developing new skills.[4]

In my survey, views on the *importance* of growth were divided as this table shows:

Freedom	Valued most by	Valued less by
Growth	Younger and more junior employees; women.	Senior leaders; men, especially at senior levels; workers aged 55+.

The priority placed on growth by the younger generation in work is borne out by external research: development opportunities are more important to Millennials when applying to a job compared to Generation Xers and Baby Boomers.[†] Gen Zers are similarly hungry for growth and progression; if they're gaining valuable skills for the future they're more than twice as likely to stay with you. They're right to be so resolute: time spent early in our career with an organization that truly prioritizes learning and development is one of the most influential factors determining our longer-term prospects.[5]

While many of us may be concerned to secure tomorrow, we also want to feel motivated at work today; we're more engaged in our jobs when we're picking up something new because that discomfort of the new keeps us more attentive and more focused. Difficult work which stretches us intellectually adds to our job satisfaction, provided there is sufficient clarity and support alongside the challenge. Yes, working on cutting-edge issues and business needs when there isn't an established process or solution in place can feel stressful at times; it also requires extra effort or longer hours. But when people are deploying their skills to the max, supporting one another, and seeing a pot of gold – positive outcomes – at the end of the rainbow then happiness ratings go up.

In my research, people's *experience* of having the freedom to grow varied as shown below.

Freedom	Experienced most by	Experienced less by
Growth	Men; employees aged under 35; white employees; remote- and hybrid-workers.	Office-based workers; Black, Asian and mixed-race employees.

The benefits of personal and professional growth aren't limited to the individual; it allows us to give more back, benefiting others

[†] Baby Boomers were born between 1946–1964, Generation X between 1965–1980, Millennials/Gen Y between 1981–1996, and Gen Z between 1997–2012.

and the businesses we work for. As one global executive observed to me, 'the more people can challenge themselves outside of their comfort zone, use the different sides of their brain and their different passions, it absolutely benefits the business'. Bringing cross-functional groups of people together for a few hours a week to think creatively about a challenge facing the business is one effective way to help people grow 'on the job'. The conversation broadens out thanks to the multiplicity of technical skills represented in the room, and participants learn to evaluate and explore a challenge from different perspectives. This enhances people's contribution and performance in their day job, which in turn makes the business stronger.

Learning and Development (L&D) functions within an organization have traditionally been viewed as a cost but, in these ways, they can indirectly generate revenue too. Companies with advanced L&D programmes have been identified as having higher employee attraction, engagement, and retention while development-focused organizations are more likely to see an increase in business revenues.

Pandora's box

We saw above how if people are getting the professional growth they want, they're more likely to stay. And therein lies the problem: 'if'.

While most of us value learning opportunities, only half of us say we're getting these. Individual development is the top driver of joy at work but on average we spend just a small fraction of our time on it – and significantly more on admin.[6] High grind, low growth is not a good recipe, and those who aren't learning are likely to be the first to leave. 'I felt stifled, I wasn't doing my best work or achieving, so I ended up doing the bare minimum and becoming disengaged' said one professional reflecting on a past low-growth experience.

Partly this is about us using our own agency: we face the paradox whereby staying inside our comfort zones might mean a less stressful work life but it also limits our opportunity to acquire fresh perspectives and new approaches that can help us respond to unfamiliar situations or challenges. When we stick to our comfort zones, we're unlikely to put ourselves 'out there' to find out what else is on offer in our organization, or to open up conversations about this with our manager or HR. If we're unclear about what a potential career path and timeline might look like, we can ask our manager for a 'career check-in' and gather some useful intelligence by chatting to other people in interesting roles about how they got to where they are today.

Partly it's about the organization, not us. How do we grow? By doing stuff we're not yet good at. But here's the trap: we're recruited into a role and expected to be competent but then we become known for certain skills and types of work and we don't get considered for others. Employers can avoid this Pandora's box by offering growth opportunities such as stretch assignments, additional lateral responsibilities, cross-functional projects, shadowing, and secondments. You also need to *show* people how they can cultivate new skills and career experiences and have regular conversations with them about this. If you don't, people take matters into their own hands and that's detrimental to workforce stability.

Even if people are highly self-motivated, actively pushing for development and brokering all the right conversations, they can still bump up against invisible, unyielding glass ceilings. Growth can stall as a result of unconscious bias, unfair processes or criteria, skewed value systems, and misguided mindsets. There's an invisible barrier in many organizations, which one CEO described to me as a 'permafrost', where people encounter those limits and get stuck. This permafrost will endure for as long as we reward fit and polish over performance and potential, and until we broaden out narrow definitions of what it takes to succeed 'around here'.

By mistakenly seeing the individual as the problem rather than the biased process or decision-making, we're failing to help people to reach their potential. I'll explore more of these barriers in the next chapter.

Career adhesives

I started my career as a graduate management trainee at Harrods, joining a 12-month programme of job rotations, shadowing opportunities, and formal training courses. My first placement was in the Wines and Spirits department in the run-up to Christmas where I experienced a baptism of fire, a hugely fun team and hands down the best work Christmas party ever. One big headache, aside from the post-party hangover, was the clawback clause in my employment contract stipulating that if I failed to see out a second-year post-programme, I had to pay back an eye-watering portion of the programme costs. Golden handcuffs like this still exist today; however forward-looking employers are deploying more enticing ways to bind talented individuals to the organization longer-term by enabling them to realize their professional aspirations.

These organizations don't think in terms of career ladders but career portfolios where employees can accumulate a diverse range of experiences that fulfils *their* appetite to collect CV-enhancing skills and roles and *the employer's* need for home-grown, flexible talent. Similarly, businesses are transcending traditional organizational or employment boundaries to facilitate mutually rewarding work opportunities. Early careers cohorts may enjoy direct access to senior leaders through shadowing, reverse-mentoring, and mirror board initiatives, along with carefully curated programmes of events to inspire their career dreams. One organization I spoke to actively encourages their younger workers to go on secondments instead of obsessing about how to retain them at all costs. After two years they go to work in another organization for a year or work freelance; those that return do so with greater maturity and valuable experience under their belts, making this strategy a win-win for both parties.

Similarly, internal jobs boards offering short-term project involvement and temporary stints in other functions can help satisfy people's appetite to learn and in the process, reduce their likelihood of leaving; at the two-year mark, an employee who has moved laterally has a greater chance of staying than someone who hasn't. AI-enabled tools are powering global internal 'talent marketplaces' where skills are mapped to current roles, future business needs, and individuals' ambitions. Employees can find out what skills they need to advance, access resources and opportunities to strengthen these, and extend their network. Adopters including General Mills, UBS, Sun Life, Google, Schneider Electric, and Mastercard report seeing positive returns such as: employees owning their careers more proactively; greater cross-functional innovation; improved internal mobility; better corporate knowledge retention; increased engagement; and reduced attrition.

As internal boundaries are dissolving, so too are external ones as businesses look to marry external talent with internal capability. The consulting firm PwC's Talent Exchange engages outside experts to work alongside their own teams, while law firm A&O Shearman's adjunct business Peerpoint provides alumni with access to A&O client work on an interim basis, delighting their clients and those lawyers seeking a career more on their own terms.

Finally, personal development objectives have long existed but have typically been overshadowed by their louder sibling, individual performance objectives; growth-focused organizations insist on both sets of objectives being met throughout the year. Being good at one's job – or overshooting one's performance targets – isn't sufficient; if the employee has lagged on their development objectives, it impacts their end of year evaluation, their rewards and their progression.

Advice for leaders

There's a vast ocean of talent management, training, and development service providers vying to support your employees' professional growth; the recommendations below are about what *you personally* can do to signal that everyone is encouraged to expand their skills and grow their careers in your organization and to role model this.

1. *Relatable stories.* Talk in an accessible, personal way about how *you've* taken advantage of opportunities to expand your skills and acquire new career experiences. Share your story of 'how I got here', your mistakes and learnings and advice you would give your younger self.

2. *Start with yes.* Say yes as much as possible to employees' specific requests for growth, looking together at ways to make this work rather than reasons to say no. Some of my most valuable career learning has come from more tangential opportunities that weren't classified as 'core' or 'on the job' training.

3. *Mind the gaps.* Look across your workforce to see who's falling under the growth radar: what are you offering for your long-tenure employees? Your ambitious cohort? Those seeking breadth rather than depth? Those making a big step up such as a first-time manager or first-time manager of managers?

4. *Mix it up.* Bring people together in unusual ways because as Matthew Syed writes in *Rebel Ideas*, the best ideas – and growth opportunities – come from 'recombinant innovation' where different fields and disciplines fuse together. Try cross-functional and even cross-industry challenges, novel pairings for events and formal 'buddies' across business units.

5. *Make time.* How can you help people free up time to reflect, assimilate learning, let minds wander, and do some blue-sky thinking? Talk about how *you* find time for

this in your busy schedule and invite others to join you in a regular, unhurried thinking session.

Advice for individuals

To engineer more freedom to grow in your current role and organization, the steps below will help you clarify what great growth looks like for you and how you're going to realize this.

1. *Interview yourself.* What are you most valued for in your team and organization? What time do you/can you carve out for your own growth? How much are you putting yourself 'out there' and signalling your appetite for growth to others?

2. *Get curious.* What opportunities are your peers accessing? Are these open to you too? If the answer is unclear, raise your observations with your manager or a mentor. Ask people in interesting roles 'what helped you get here?'.

3. *Sort your squad.* Look at who you tend to associate with – is it time to refresh or expand your network? In her book *WorkJoy*, talent expert Beth Stallwood recommends building a diverse 'squad' where people in your network actively support your growth by fulfilling one of six squad roles from cheerleader to challenger.

4. *Plan your progression.* Jot down your work goals for one, three and five years' time, then identify the skills, experiences and contacts you'll need to acquire or strengthen. Next, note down specific development activities you will undertake and finally plot how you'll ask squad members to support you.

5. *Make it happen.* Real growth takes graft, so seek out an informal sponsor, find a mentor or set up a co-mentoring pair with a work friend, buddy up with a 'thinking partner',‡ ask your manager for more frequent, light-touch

---

‡ A concept and practice introduced by Nancy Kline in her book *Time to Think: Listening to ignite the human mind.*

development check-ins, and drop your progression goals into as many conversations as possible.

A stable base

In psychologist Abraham Maslow's Hierarchy of Needs, safety comes before self-actualization. This means that in order to attend effectively to our professional and personal growth, we have to first feel secure in our context. In the next chapter, I'll explore the third freedom: our freedom to be ourselves at work, to be accepted by others for who we are and valued for what we bring.

Chapter 9
Self-expression

'I disapprove of what you say, but I will defend to the death your right to say it.'

Evelyn Beatrice Hall

I hear you, I see you

HOW OFTEN HAVE you witnessed aggression in the workplace? Aside from one very shouty manager early in my career who had clearly signed up to Douglas McGregor's Theory X of management (recall Chapter 5), very fortunately my answer would be 'rarely'. Undoubtedly that has been partly down to luck and privilege, but since 1999, we've also witnessed the concept of psychological safety, coined by Harvard professor Amy Edmondson, enter the mainstream of conversations about work and become a strategic imperative for organizations looking to attract and retain high-quality employees and harness their full potential. In parallel, over the last two decades movements such as #MeToo and Black Lives Matter exposing other forms of aggression and prejudice in the workplace have gained global attention while courageous whistleblowers have laid bare the toxic, repressive work cultures at the heart of high-profile corporate scandals at Enron, Wirecard, Theranos, Uber, and other organizations.

In this chapter, I'll unpack the third freedom of self-expression and explore its different nuances from psychological safety to belonging and diversity of thought. You'll discover how highly people value working in organizations that give humanity and profit-making equal weight, and the substantial business benefits that come from fostering a work culture founded on respect, inclusivity and openness. I'll look at what happens when people are denied the freedom of self-expression and then turn to some positive ways organizations can promote this freedom.

Speaking up

Ask people what freedom of self-expression means to them, and you'll hear recurring themes such as:

Not being afraid to speak up.

Sharing my ideas openly and contributing to discussions.

Feeling that my voice and opinions are heard.

Knowing I'll be listened to and acknowledged.

For people to share their ideas without fear of criticism or humiliation, there needs to be a culture of trust and openness where people feel comfortable and confident to say what they think. Have you ever been on a call or in a meeting where you've raised your hand and volunteered a suggestion or a point of view, only for someone to look at you or comment in a disparaging way, or swiftly pass over your contribution? This type of behaviour discourages us from speaking up again next time.

Freedom of self-expression also encompasses freedom of thought where people are encouraged to think outside the box and express different opinions, unconstrained by intellectual or political orthodoxies or one 'right way to think'. Don't equate a psychologically safe culture with niceness: the latter prioritizes comfort and collusion over candour and challenge to the detriment of individual and team effectiveness. Making it safe for people to speak up means inviting diverging points of views, having healthy (and respectful) debates, giving and receiving constructive feedback, and agreeing to disagree when needed.

If you see your best ideas stolen by others, your points of view manipulated for someone else's gain, or your own beliefs and perspectives undermined by gaslighting* behaviour, then caution takes over. A psychologically safe environment emboldens people to take risks, make and admit mistakes, and learn from failures.

Psychological safety is a *collective* effort that needs to be authorized by leaders, managers, and peers; without this secure foundation and active, ongoing support, people's freedom to express themselves will quickly falter. Equally we each bear responsibility to moderate our language and behaviour in the interests of the group's positive functioning: as one professional observed to me:

> Sometimes you have to be diplomatic at work and not say what you think, as in life generally. It can feel frustrating but a good work environment requires a degree of conscious self-censorship.

Belonging

According to Bill Gates, if he met a time traveller from the future, the one question he would ask them would be 'are humans thriving?'.[1]

As well as to grow, flourish, and be successful, to thrive also means to feel at home – to feel like we belong. When we belong, we experience an emotional connection with others around us; we feel valued, understood, accepted, and respected. People who

* Tricking or controlling someone by making them believe untruths or doubting themselves.

are thriving at work are more likely to say they are treated with respect and that they smile and laugh frequently.[2]

Without this emotional connection with colleagues, work becomes functional and transactional, at best a means to an end and at worst, a lonely soul-sapping ordeal. Are workers around the globe generally thriving at work? No, as Figure 5 drawing on research by Gallup shows.

Underlining the importance of belonging and appreciation, consulting firm McKinsey & Co found that that half of employees who recently left their jobs attributed their three top reasons for leaving as:

1. Not feeling valued by their organizations.
2. Not feeling valued by their managers.
3. Feeling like they didn't belong.[3]

Figure 5 How people are feeling in their work lives

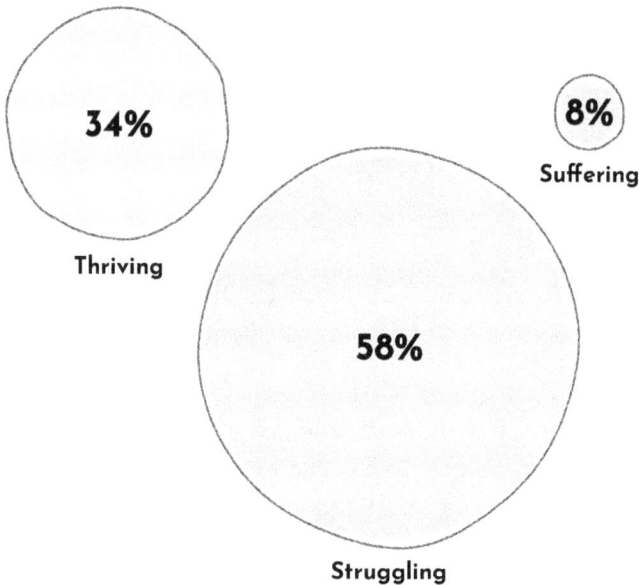

Just as psychological safety is a collective effort, so too is belonging. By paying attention to interpersonal dynamics, being curious and open to learning more about each other, and approaching potentially uncomfortable situations in a non-judgemental way instead of avoiding them or apportioning blame, teams can cultivate a greater sense of belonging where different personalities and perspectives can flourish. And that's good for business: teams with thriving workers see significantly lower absenteeism, turnover, accidents, and higher customer loyalty.

Why self-expression matters

With freedom to express themselves, people enjoy their jobs more and they're generally happier. As one professional shared ruefully:

> I've spent a lot of time with companies that want you to conform to a 'type'. Finding an employer where you can be accepted with your true personality brings the best out of you.

Regarding self-moderating our communication and behaviour when we're at work, keeping our stronger forms of expression and emotions in check pays off in terms of the work environment. With the well-researched phenomenon of emotional contagion, emotions spread rapidly across teams and organizations even in virtual settings. As one law partner put it to me:

> Being able to call out the superstar jerks, egotistical bad eggs and mood-hoovers makes coming into the office a pleasure. I'd much rather have nicer colleagues than a prettier place to sit.

Freedom of self-expression also results in people putting in discretionary effort. When we feel heard and we feel we belong, we are *empowered* to perform at our best and we are far more likely to say we're *doing* our best work. These positive consequences extend to the business' performance as well. Being listened to results in organizations making better decisions and bringing products to market more swiftly. Organizations that embrace diversity are more likely to see above-average profitability and outperform less diverse organizations on profitability.

Speaking up also enables businesses to manage risk better: as a leader, you may not be aware of something that's happening downstream or on the front line, and this creates blind spots on your radar. If you want people to *speak up*, as a leader you need to be skilled (and ideally trained) in how to *listen up*. Showing you've heard – by going back with a response, keeping people updated and/or taking action – is equally important because if people raise information to you and then nothing happens, they may not bother to speak up a second time. When leaders, by their own example, show what 'doing the right thing' looks like, then speaking up becomes normalized and problems can bubble up to the surface early before these intensify. A risk and compliance leader explained to me:

> Speaking up and whistleblowing are on the same scale, they're just at opposite ends. Whistleblowing is your nuclear option when everything has gone wrong, whereas 'speaking up' is dealing with problems right from the beginning.

Finally, expressing one's views is crucial for innovation to happen; without this, the brilliant thoughts brewing in people heads go nowhere. In a culture that welcomes everyone's perspectives, leaders can more easily crowdsource ideas, tap into subject matter experts and drive collaboration across the organization. Equally, leaders gain honest feedback about what's *not* working, building organizational confidence in the robustness of plans.

Snapshots of self-expression

From my own research, self-expression was fairly evenly spread out across the *importance* rankings but mattered more to certain groups:

Freedom	Valued most by	Valued less by
Self-expression	Younger employees, women, other under-represented groups and office-based workers.	Men, senior leaders, remote workers.

The younger cohort indicated a higher focus on psychological safety compared to older age groups, but this was also reported at mid-career level too.

In terms of people's *experiences* of having the freedom to express themselves without fear of reprisal or judgement, the picture is as follows:

Freedom	Experienced most by	Experienced less by
Self-expression	Men; older employees.	Women; Asian, Black and mixed-race employees; employees aged 35–44; senior leaders.

Female respondents made frequent mention of not being able to fully express opinions, being talked over or feeling silenced; in contrast, few male respondents reported such difficulties. Meanwhile, Asian, Black, and mixed-race respondents, as a combined group, cited managers who discouraged them from speaking up or venturing out of their lane. At the top of organizations, people in leadership roles often feeling less psychologically safe, and in Chapter 13 I look more closely at some of the reasons behind this.

Voice vacuums

In my mid-20s I was asked in an interview if I was the same person *at* work as *outside* of work. I hesitated, then trepidatiously answered 'no', explaining that I became my 'professional self' at work (I got the job, read into that what you will). Apparently I wasn't alone in presenting a certain way in order to fit in; while managers overwhelmingly see their organization as inclusive, reality for many is very different with 45% of workers saying they've had to change something about themselves to get on in the workplace.[4] This percentage increases for minority individuals, particularly Black employees and people from the LGBTQ+ community. One straight, white male commented to me 'I am lucky as, having privilege, I have always felt relatively free to be myself and people have encouraged me to speak up'; in contrast, an Asian female shared 'I'm not able to express my views: managers tend to talk over me or ask me to stop talking.' Another study found Gen Z are cautious about being themselves around colleagues and finding their voice at work, hesitating to speak with managers about wellbeing or personal issues.[5] These insights indicate that many people do not feel comfortable expressing themselves authentically at work and this often leads to reduced job satisfaction, mental wellbeing, performance, and collaboration.

One Asian female executive shared with me her experiences of exclusive or unsupportive behaviours:

> When I look back at where I've done very well, it was because of the right combination of people at the right time who were open-minded enough to get on with everybody else in the team. But if you happen to have one rotten apple, that is very damaging, and the speed at which the cohesiveness of a team can be damaged by one person in a team surprised me, even if that team had previously gelled well together.

As Steve Gruenert and Todd Whitaker state in *School Culture Rewired* 'the culture of any organization is shaped by the worst behaviour the leader is willing to tolerate'. Accepting even mild anti-social or prejudiced behaviours jeopardizes people's freedom of self-expression and consequently retention: a toxic corporate culture is the strongest predictor of attrition, ten times more significant than compensation.[6] And the damage lingers post-exit, as one professional explained: 'My manager, a group HRD, gaslighted me constantly; I ended up with poor mental health, crushed confidence and left. It felt like I had much to prove in my next role.'

Another commented 'the area I see most silenced of late is voice – psychological safety and grumpy managers rarely coexist'. One in four of us are likely to experience at least one instance of conflict in a twelve-month period and employees who experience conflict are less positive about their manager's ability to seek their opinions, keep them informed and allow them to influence decisions – in other words, to express themselves.

A secure base

To develop a psychologically safe culture, we can turn back to child development psychology and John Bowlby's concept of a 'secure base' drawn from attachment theory. The secure base is the safe zone in which the child explores, forms relationships with others and grows in independence. Translating this to organizations, 'secure base leaders … provide a sense of safety that allows employees to take risks, learn from failures and perform at their best',[7] in contrast to unpredictable or inconsistent leadership that fires employees' anxiety and self-preservation instincts. Later on, Roy Baumeister and Mark Leary's 'need to belong' theory clarified that our sense of safety comes as much from our relationships with colleagues as with our leaders.

A hallmark of a psychologically safe environment is mutual respect; this is also the stand-out predictor of how positive an organization's culture is and what would persuade the 'quiet quitters' – 59% of the global workforce – to actively re-engage, specifically more approachable managers with whom they can talk openly and who respect them more.

Developing a secure base starts in recruitment where interviewers can ask questions that encourage self-expression like 'what makes you tick?', 'what will we learn about you in six months' time?' and 'what did you like most/least about your last work culture?', Next, ditch the traditional onboarding approach where typically employers overwhelm their new employees with a tidal wave of information, conveniently ignoring the reality that in the rush to fill their heads most of those details will likely be forgotten by those new joiners before their first day is over. Far more effective is to whittle the mammoth list down to ten essential things people most need to know to help them land positively, feel good about their early days in your organization and negotiate their identity successfully in their new environment. You're aiming to help people to feel as quickly as possible like their feet are on solid ground and they belong, instead of paddling furiously to keep their heads above water.

Let personalities shine and ensure you have a variety of mechanisms and resources to regularly gauge how openly people can express themselves; at one creative marketing agency managers receive 360° feedback on their ability to connect with and support team members while Atlassian deploys tools like the Team Health Monitor and the Trust Battery, for example.[8] Finally, make it easy for people to press the 'red button' when exclusive, belittling, or manipulative behaviours undermine openness and respect.

Advice for leaders

Research by world-renowned organizational culture expert Edgar Schein, shared in his 1985 book, *Organizational Culture and Leadership*, found that the most critical factors influencing an organization's culture are:

1. Leader attention, measurement, rewards, and control.
2. Leader reaction to critical incidents.
3. Leader role modelling and coaching.

With that in mind, consider the following practices to encourage others to speak up, express their views and let their personalities shine:

1. *Ask 'how are you?' three times* to get past superficial niceties to an honest answer, and don't ask unless you truly have the time to listen.

2. *Invite people to disclose more about themselves* with questions like 'what do you care about outside of work?', 'what do you want to have a shot at in life?', and 'how can we best support you?'.

3. *Bring your own lived experiences into your conversations* so people see you as an individual and share their own stories in return.

4. *Try Jeff Bezos' habit of speaking last in meetings* and inviting the most junior person to speak first, to avoid influencing people too early and to elicit all the views represented around the table.

5. *Ask simple questions that solicit richer information and encourage critical thinking.* In their book *Collective Intelligence: how to build a business that's smarter than you,* board advisors and business leaders Pippa Begg and Jennifer Sundberg suggest 'what, why, so what, now what?'.

6. *Try breaking a taboo or two* by broaching conversations about things that rarely get acknowledged or mentioned. People will notice and follow your own behaviour, bringing a wider range of topics and views out into the open.

Advice for individuals

Every day we are evaluating how secure we feel in our environment and in response, moderating how we express ourselves, and we all share responsibility for creating a psychologically safe culture. Below are three recommendations for expressing yourself more freely, transcending biases and barriers and having respectful, empathetic two-way exchanges.

1. *Discover the essential human needs that underpin every interaction we have.* In *Why Weren't we Taught this at School?*, former barrister and CEO Alice Sheldon draws on non-violent communication principles to explain how to speak and listen in ways that feel more authentic, resolve conflict and enrich our relationships.

2. *Build a diverse community around you.* While 'finding your tribe' is about connecting with people like you, this is about seeking out difference. Nurture relationships with people who bring contrasting perspectives, who can challenge your narrative and illuminate potential blindspots about how you're coming across to others. On blindspots, the JoHari window is an excellent framework for enhancing your self-awareness and interpersonal communication.

3. *Practice strategies for dealing with negative emotions during stress or conflict.* First, notice how the emotion is manifesting in you then allow it to wash away, not overwhelm you. Second, tune in to what the emotion is signalling about what's important to you. Finally, consider your choices for how you might respond.

Moving on to meaning

In the next chapter, I'll examine the fourth freedom: our freedom to get on with meaningful work. Many negative expressions and aphorisms convey the drudgery, pointlessness, and frustrations of work, from 'wading through treacle' and 'pushing water uphill' to 'spinning plates', 'moving the goal posts', and 'rearranging deckchairs'. Find out how people are seeking fit-for-purpose organizations and more effective ways of working where they can immerse themselves in interesting and impactful work.

Chapter 10
Meaningful work

'Far and away the best prize that life offers is the chance to work hard at work worth doing.'

Theodore Roosevelt

Visions and vexations

WHETHER OR NOT you agree with Roosevelt's virtuous statement, the vast majority of us work in order to earn enough to pay our bills and provide for ourselves and our loved ones. Some jobs may be more vocational in nature than others but whatever industry we're in and whatever our role and pay grade, many of us hope that work is more than simply a functional means to an end. We look to our work lives to provide us with a sense of purpose, to draw meaning from our daily endeavours, to make a positive impact in society in some way. For me, the meaning that has spurred me on in my career has been about helping to create better-functioning teams and organizations where people can thrive and do their best work.

This chapter takes a closer look at what meaningful work is and what it represents to others, and assesses what gets in the way of focusing on our core roles, from competing priorities and rammed calendars to distractions and poorly designed environments. I'll look at how AI is impacting the way people spend their working hours and how our freedom to pursue meaningful work is compromised by bureaucracy, boredom, presenteeism, performative theatre, and other unconstructive characteristics of our world of work.

Purposeful not pointless

If you've ever worked a job which felt pointless, you'll know how demotivating and frustrating this can be. Doing meaningful work matters deeply to people; a survey of over 2,500 US working adults 93% believed it was very or somewhat important to do a job that was meaningful.[1]

What does 'meaningful' actually mean?

Is it work that is pro-social in nature, in other words that contributes to improving people's lives and social outcomes? Or is it work that gives us a personal sense of growth and self-realization? In fact, both answers are true, but they don't necessarily have to hold true at the same time.[2] Your job can serve some social good but you might still feel frustrated by or disappointed with your role, the nature of your day-to-day work tasks or your interactions with colleagues. Conversely, you might feel satisfyingly stretched and motivated because you're acquiring new skills and doing interesting work in a field or discipline that fascinates you, but that work might not contribute to the improvement of people's lives – it may even have a negative impact on health, democracy, the environment or society more broadly, for example, in tobacco marketing, fast fashion operations, gambling operations, and online disinformation.

How many of us experience meaningful work?

Or is this just the preserve of a fortunate few, with the majority of us stuck in unrewarding, unfulfilling roles and longing for a better work life? Despite the popular concept of 'bullshit jobs' introduced by sociologist David Graeber in 2013 which posited that many modern jobs were pointless and even damaging to people, more recent research has disproved this. In the UK, a team of researchers has consistently tracked people's experiences of meaningful work via the national Skills and Employment Survey that has been conducted every four years since 1986, with over 29,000 respondents in its 2024 survey. They have found that only 5% doubted the value of their work and a whopping majority of 75% consistently reported believing they were doing useful work.[3]

What drives meaningful work?

We derive – or assign – meaning to our work through our continuous experience of work; in a nutshell, it's about our sense of fit and fulfilment. It is also subjective, varying by individual, and it stems from a range of sources. Broadly, meaning is determined by the following factors:

- The characteristics of our job such as task variety and agency over how we work.
- The quality of our interpersonal relationships with co-workers.
- A sense of belonging and community, not simply a focus on ourselves.
- The feeling of doing useful work that makes a positive impact in some way.
- Using our skills and acquiring new ones.
- How central work is to our life overall.
- Having a supportive manager.
- Having a say in broader organizational matters that may impact us.
- Leaders who help us to see how we contribute to the organization's goals and achievements.

Pay *isn't* a driver of meaning and this finding is consistent across all job types. Likewise, uncertainty, organizational change and work pressure don't have a significant impact on our sense of meaning at work. We can find our job extremely challenging, difficult to do or even distressing but still feel that it is meaningful and worth doing.

Finding meaning at work contributes directly to positive outcomes for us individually by giving us a greater sense of satisfaction with work and life, improved wellbeing and reduced stress, for example. It also contributes to positive outcomes for the organizations we work for, such as a more motivated, engaged, and productive workforce that is more committed, less likely to leave, more creative, and better at sharing knowledge.

Meaning as a freedom

In my conversations with people while writing this book, when I asked them what freedom at work meant to them, few spontaneously mentioned the freedom to get on with meaningful work. When I prompted about this specifically, people usually concluded that this was indeed important to them – they just hadn't necessarily considered it to be a 'freedom' before. The question gave them a new perspective on their priorities and experiences at work.

In my quantitative research, people in fact ranked meaningful work as their second most *important* freedom overall, behind autonomy. They commented:

> The work I do has to mean something; I want to make a difference.

> Having a sense of purpose is the single most important motivation for me.

> I work on issues of national strategic importance and I can see how the policies we design bring positive outcomes for consumers and the environment.

I care about what we are trying to do and about leaving things in good shape for the next generation of colleagues coming along.

I want to be more conscious and more intentional about making an impact on people's lives.

Some groups valued the freedom to do meaningful work more than others:

Freedom	Valued most by	Valued less by
Meaningful work	Senior leaders and managers, office-based workers, men and mid-career women.	Younger employees, particularly younger women.

This suggests that as we near the later chapter(s) of our working lives or the peaks of our career trajectories, we value making an impact more than other factors. When we're newer to the world of work, making progress along our chosen career paths and acquiring skills and experience appears to be a greater priority.

With meaningful work, people will compromise on other aspects of freedom if their organization's mission is compelling enough:

If you believe in the 'big picture' goal, it's less important if some elements of day-to-day tasks aren't so meaningful.

The overall goal of the organization makes the lack of some of the other freedoms acceptable.

There needs to be a close enough match between the business' priorities and what individual employees care about; in other words, a sense of alignment between self and organization. Often, 'meaningful work' equates to serving customers well but if messages from leaders are mostly about chasing sales or reducing costs, for example, then that disconnect in what is valued can cause people to re-evaluate their commitment. Plus, employees who are clear about the priorities are far more likely to decide to stay put for at least a couple of years and to say they rarely think about job hunting.[4]

Invariably there's still a negotiation between the needs of the business and people's particular interests; handled well, this can lead to exploratory projects, side hustles, and role adjustments with the potential to benefit employer and employee alike. Adobe's Kickbox programme provides employees with the tools, time, and resources to develop new ideas and is openly shared externally. 3M's 15% Culture encourages employees to use some of their working hours to pursue innovative ideas that excite them. The boss of one wavering HR Director I spoke with encouraged her to incorporate into her role her passion for supporting students into employment, so she set up three work experience programmes and a mentoring scheme, turning down offers to move elsewhere.

Demented butterflies

Even when motivated by your organization's goals, people's freedom to get on with meaningful work is undermined by the nature of working life today. The inordinate volume of calls and meetings, incoming messages and the chopping up of our working hours into 'time confetti'* by our incessant switching between conversations, tasks, programmes, and devices severely impact our productivity. It has become extremely hard to preserve 'focus' time, maintain our attention for an extended stretch or to do the deep thinking that strategic or creative insights require. We've become demented butterflies, flitting at speed from interaction to task, rarely pausing to delve beyond the superficial.

In research for my first book, *The Future of Time*, professionals told me that 'dealing with incoming demands day-to-day' and 'participating in calls and meetings' consumed most of their weekly hours; they needed upwards of eight to ten hours of

* A term coined by Brigid Schulte.

focus time but averaged as little as one to three hours. To get the important work done they had to go 'off grid', get up even earlier and work in their own time.

Meeting volumes shot up during the pandemic and have barely subsided since; Microsoft's analysis of Teams usage reports a significant increase in overlapping meetings and almost half of meeting participants multi-tasking. People are sleepwalking through their meetings, accepting them as a necessary evil. If instead we looked more closely at how we use meetings at work and how we run them, then we can potentially transform not only how we feel about our work but how effectively we get work done. Introducing meeting-free days is one option, but it's also about being more intentional about what meetings are for, how they are run, how people contribute in them, and calling out ineffective meeting habits.

Partly thanks to all these meetings, we're locked in a permanent pandemic of busyness where only some of that activity is ultimately impactful and a large portion is 'work about work'. Management guru John Kotter termed this 'false urgency' in his 2008 book, *A Sense of Urgency*, and it hasn't diminished today. Many workers find themselves mired in 'busy work' – seemingly productive activity that doesn't contribute to meaningful results – which consumes vast swathes of their daily or weekly workload.

Bureaucracy, the internal processes and structures that gird decision-making, power and control, is intended to manage co-ordination and risk but often slows progress and stifles innovation. In a Fortune interview healthcare and agriculture multinational Bayer's CEO Bill Anderson described how:

> Bureaucracy has put Bayer in a stranglehold. Our internal rules for employees span 1,362 pages. We have excellent people [...] but they are trapped in 12 levels of hierarchy. [...] To succeed, we need an environment where people and their ideas can thrive – not be stymied by red tape.

They have embarked on a mission to eliminate rules and bureaucracy and put '95% of decision-making in the hands of the people actually doing the work.' In a model termed Dynamic Shared Ownership, they are stripping out organizational layers, reducing manager numbers, and replacing annual budgets with '90-day sprints by self-directed teams'.[5]

Accompanying busyness and bureaucracy is the tsunami of communication breaking over employees via multiple channels. Leaders acknowledge the 'white noise' of communication while the biggest complaint in most companies regarding internal communication is overwhelm: an endless, relentless stream of updates and reply-all's that workers have to wade through each and every day. Every organization is having to figure out how to cut through the clutter to curate and disseminate relevant information in a way that's manageable, absorbable, and engaging for people.

Fostering FOMO

CEOs who want to bring people back to the office more frequently cite a desire (or need) to strengthen creativity, culture, and connection. But an office characterized by open-plan rows of desks and cubicles just doesn't enable those three Cs; instead, it harks back to the old school 'manager as supervisor' philosophy. Neither does it enable focused work because everyone's on virtual calls; in a poll of 1,000 office workers by British retailer Currys, chatty colleagues were cited as the biggest source of distraction, followed by internet issues and mobile phone usage.[6] To help them get on with meaningful work, people want more equitable access to natural light, greenery, and a variety of spaces that support different work activities: informal areas with comfortable seating for discussions with colleagues or solo work amidst a co-working/café-style buzz; quiet zones for deep, uninterrupted work; enclosed spaces for confidential conversations; collaborative hubs for project teams and brainstorming. Most importantly, people want to see their close colleagues and friends on their in-office days. Get these factors right, and FOMO (the fear of missing out) will draw people willingly back in.

There is a new appreciation that office design is about helping people to do their work well and rebuilding social capital. Office spaces *can* be inspirational again; the secret to getting people working together in-person again on a regular basis is to create an environment where they enjoy being there and experience the benefits directly. While you can't cater to every individual's personal preferences, you can find out how the office's configuration and characteristics can, broadly speaking, better meet the needs of the people who use it regularly. Taking this employee-centric approach will enable you to design a space that offers a much better experience of work; in turn this can help improve business performance and profitability.

Goodbye daily grind?

In the past, our freedom to do meaningful work has been eroded by time-consuming tasks such as repetitive or low-value-adding activities, painstaking analyses, drafting and re-drafting, editing and reviewing of materials and reports. We're on the cusp – possibly past the tipping point – of consigning that to history with the roll-out of generative AI tools and large language models in organizations; by 2030, it is estimated that some 70% of companies will have adopted at least one type of AI technology.[7]

AI tools allow us to handle large data sets, work more efficiently, speed up response times, reduce human error, and tailor solutions to the individual, plus far more besides. In theory this will free up more time for people to focus on the longer-term, more developmental- and relationship-oriented aspects of work. People's present experiences of AI and leaders' expectations of AI in the future can broadly be summarized as shown in Figure 6.

Figure 6 AI today and tomorrow

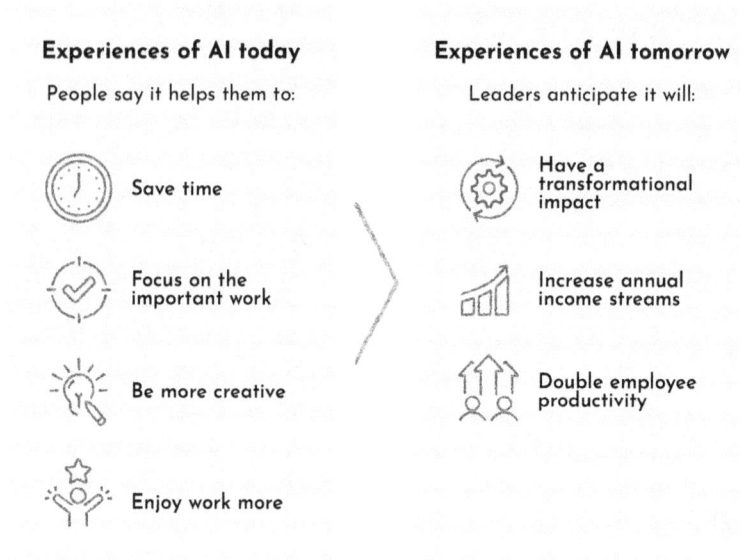

Experiences of AI today	Experiences of AI tomorrow
People say it helps them to:	Leaders anticipate it will:

Experiences of AI today
People say it helps them to:

- Save time
- Focus on the important work
- Be more creative
- Enjoy work more

Experiences of AI tomorrow
Leaders anticipate it will:

- Have a transformational impact
- Increase annual income streams
- Double employee productivity

AI's impact is likely to be felt unevenly, but for the organizations and individuals ready to explore and embrace it, it promises the potential to release us from the more tedious, less enjoyable aspects of daily work.

When meaning fades

Shakespeare's famous line 'all the world's a stage, and all the men and women merely players' from *As You Like It* applies equally to the world of work as to other spheres of life. Even those fortunate to feel fulfilled by purposeful, engaging, and intellectually stretching careers have encountered at some point the unappealing characteristics of work such as presenteeism (turning up for work for the sake of being seen to be in, rather than working purposefully), performative work (striving to give the appearance of being busy and productive while accomplishing little), mindless routines, boredom and burnout that diminish the meaning we draw from our work lives. As with *importance*, meaningful work was ranked second when

I surveyed people's *experience* of the four freedoms. Men ranked it slightly lower than women and the under 35s rated it their least experienced freedom, suggesting they struggle to find meaning in work especially in corporate environments.

One professional described the freedom to do meaningful work to me as 'being valued for your contribution and measured by your results rather than your time physically at the office'. Yet according to HR leaders, presenteeism has been rising among employees who work from home for some of the week, including still working when ill, while 42% women say they are judged on the hours they are present or online rather than their outputs.[8] The proliferation of activity tracking tools described in Chapter 5 have generated a new set of presenteeism behaviours, from coffee badging to mouse jiggling.[†] These dynamics illustrate the 'productivity paranoia' that has been documented whereby the vast majority of employees assert they are productive at work but only a small minority of leaders believe them.

Presenteeism is one example of 'performative work' that gives the impression of busyness and diligence while accomplishing nothing. In one US study an astonishing proportion of participants confessed to performative work in the preceding 12 months, with some spending ten hours or more per week on this. In the UK, just under a third of the average desk worker's day is given over to performative work. Many of us feel compelled to respond to messages quickly even out-of-hours and feel pressured to let our colleagues know we are at work and being productive.[9] More subtle are organizational 'scripts': learned language and behaviours that represent 'the way we talk or do things around here'. These can provide useful verbal shortcuts and aid our sense-making but unmonitored, they can hinder authenticity and meaningful conversations.[10]

[†] Coffee badging: swiping briefly into the office, coffee in hand, before swiftly heading home again. Mouse jiggling: simulating computer mouse movement to give the impression of work activity.

Meanwhile monotony and dull work breed boredom, which is not only an excruciating experience but a downward spiral too. Research shows we often suppress boredom at work to power through tedious tasks and objectives but this only reduces our productivity in future bored spells.[11] When the negatives of monotony outweigh the positives of community, we realize we've lost our freedom to do meaningful work and the job-hunt begins. On the other end of the spectrum to boredom and monotony are exhaustion and burnout, experiences of which have been rising fast in recent years impacting between 42% and 63% of workers today and affecting women more than men.[12] A major consequence of burnout is that people feel mentally detached from their work and derive less meaning from it.

Advice for leaders

Returning to Roosevelt's expression 'work worth doing', here are ways to engage colleagues in a dialogue about meaningful work:

1. *Invite your leadership team to articulate what 'meaningful work' is from the perspective of different stakeholders.* Five years from today, what do you want clients, colleagues, shareholders, and regulators (if relevant) to be saying about the impact your organization has had? What data would confirm this?
2. *It's hard to establish robust productivity measures in knowledge-based work but if you spot 'productivity paranoia' in your organization:*
   a. Ask what 'productive' means to each team.
   b. Explore what helps them to work productively and what hinders them.
3. *Find out if lack of focus time is damaging your business.* Ask people:
   a. How much focus time broadly do you need per week? How much do you typically get, and when?

      b.   What one thing would make it easier to focus on the important work?

4. *Equip your teams to work smarter not harder and strengthen social bonds at the same time.* In a two-hour workshop you can:

      a.   Identify what helps them to deliver the important work successfully.

      b.   Surface what's draining energy and fun or wasting working time.

      c.   Empower them to implement positive changes within their control.

5. *Consider what you want your physical workspace to do for your organization and your people.* Is it to strengthen your ability to work together? Create a greater sense of belonging? Help people to solve problems more easily? Invite people to force-rank these priorities and see how different groups of people respond.

Advice for individuals

Meaning in life and work is deeply subjective, as a guest business leader on my podcast *The Business of Being Brilliant* once articulated so eloquently: 'Who is there to judge what the race is, how long the race is? It's you. It's all up to you.'

To find meaning takes effort and agency; I believe in building regular habits that help us realize more rewarding outcomes. Try the following:

1. Look below the surface. When the rush of the work week is over, find a quiet place and ask yourself:

      a.   What has brought meaning to you?

      b.   What's missing?

      c.   How will you make more time for that in your work and home life?

2. Prioritize meaning and joy *today*. We tend to work hard today in pursuit of a better tomorrow. Think of a time recently when you left work with a spring in your step.
   a. What helped you feel like that?
   b. What can you do today that would put another spring in your step?
3. Put boundaries around your busyness. In deciding what commitments to accept or decline, Professor Hal Hershfield, author of *Your Future Self*, recommends saying yes to those that make others happy without reducing your own happiness. For low-risk ways to free up your time more meaningfully at work, use my Time ROI tool.[‡]
4. Have a genuinely exciting plan B. A dear friend and mentor gave me this invaluable advice at a difficult time in my life. By researching and putting a detailed picture together of what a compelling alternative work option could look like for you, you'll feel better prepared – and more positive – if plan A comes to an abrupt or involuntary end. This is sometimes described as the 'no lose' model for decision-making.

Making it happen

In Part 3, I've explored the four freedoms in detail: what these are, why these matter to people, and how they impact employees' decisions to stay or leave. The bigger challenge is still ahead: how to bring these freedoms to life within the confines and operating constraints of an organization that is most likely (but not necessarily) a commercial, profit-making entity. Let's turn to operationalizing freedom.

[‡] Download this at www.helenbeedham.com.

Part 4 Operationalizing freedom

'We must be free not because we claim freedom, but because we practice it.'
William Faulkner

Chapter 11
Freedom framework

'The worst enemy of life, freedom and the common decencies is total anarchy; their second worst enemy is total efficiency.'
Attributed to Aldous Huxley

Balancing act

THE REMAINING CHAPTERS set out an approach, honed through many conversations with leaders and organizational experts, for how to offer freedom as an employer. What are the different ways you can do that? How do you manage the risks and the tensions to ensure that your freedom is channelling people's energy and effort effectively and not descending into damaging anarchy?

William McKnight, the long-serving President and later Chairman of the American multinational 3M that gave us scotch tape and Post-it notes said: 'Hire good people and leave them alone. Delegate responsibility and encourage men and women to exercise their initiative'.[1] While agreeing with the essence of his statement, freedom doesn't run itself and to give people freedom, you actually need to provide a robust amount of structure. The key lies, as Aldous Huxley pinpoints, in getting this balance right;

this is not a one-time effort but a dynamic, ongoing process of experimentation, learning, discovery, and adaptation.

Risk walks hand-in-hand with freedom and at some point, any organization committed to creating People Glue may encounter an unwelcome breach of trust or act of negligence, so Chapter 12 takes an honest look at what to do when freedom falters. Chapter 13 assesses the role of the leader in an organization that embraces freedom, the challenges and vulnerabilities they face and the freedom they themselves need. In the final chapter, I turn to people managers, the critical role they play in creating glue and how they can become effective 'freedom coaches'.

Before that, in this chapter I investigate what's in the DNA of organizations that achieve freedom and high retention. The human genome is 99.6% identical across all humans, with only 0.4% variation by individual. In contrast, no single freedom template will work for all organizations and no single lever or policy will yield People Glue on its own – this is complex, highly tailored, whole systems stuff. So, the absence here of a step-by-step guide or a methodology is deliberate, instead I offer an organizing framework to help you evaluate what you already have in place and where to focus your efforts, given the nature of your business, your goals, and your workforce. This framework advocates paying attention to three key aspects of your organization: parameters, programmes, and practices.

Parameters

By parameters, I mean the things through which you as a leader create *alignment* and *accountability*; aligning your people's energy and efforts with your business goals and holding yourselves accountable for delivering what is required. Within these parameters people have freedom to operate, use their creativity, make their own decisions but critically, you're all still moving in the same direction. So, what are these parameters?

Creating alignment

First up, it's your purpose: why your organization exists and its contribution to the world. This ignites people's excitement and unites them around a shared ambition. In more granular terms, your mission articulates *what* you want to achieve and *how* you'll achieve it. Over time, as business strategy evolves in response to changing realities, watch out for your mission becoming opaque or outdated. Ultimately, you need to enable everyone to understand what you're trying to achieve.

Alongside your purpose, you create alignment through your business plan because when you operate with a high degree of freedom, you've got to make sure that the deliverables and the responsibilities are crystal clear. In tandem, your OKRs (objectives and key results) and KPIs (key performance indicators) help people see what progress you're collectively making.

One financial services organization I spoke to uses their three high-level annual OKRs to give people a track to run on and to define the boundaries of what good looks like while offering a high degree of freedom in how they get there. At a global marketing business, they similarly talk about providing 'tramlines not guardrails'. Context matters enormously: sometimes there's high demand in the market for what you are selling, creating a fair wind that blows your business along briskly towards its goals. Other times, there may be market conditions, workforce shortages, or product/service complexities that act as a headwind, slowing you down or demanding greater resource and effort. Creating a narrative to explain the context surrounding your OKRs and KPIs helps people to make sense of the data, and as a leader you can coach people in interpreting that context and determining how best to respond by asking questions like: What were you trying to achieve in this last period? What worked, what didn't? What's your view of the risks and opportunities ahead and how confident are you feeling? Given all of that, what will you stop doing, start doing, do differently?.

Creating accountability

So, your purpose and business plan with tangible metrics create *alignment*, but freedom to operate also requires *accountability* and this accountability has to be designed deep into your operating model and your business processes. I don't just mean your people management processes, but your budget discussions, your decision-making processes, your business reviews, your delegation of authority framework, your approach to risk management. You're articulating expectations for how you go about safety, quality, delivery, cost, and more, and you're holding people accountable through your business processes for working in these ways and meeting these standards. There have to be some clear 'red lines' which denote what is *not* permitted – for example in terms of how you treat customers, how you make trades or financing decisions, how you underwrite risk, how you handle people's personal data.

One CEO reflected to me that 'if the trade-off for greater freedom, greater autonomy, greater decision-making is a collective accountability, then we've found most of people have stepped up for that'. Your aim here as a leader is to maintain an adult-to-adult relationship whereby you are encouraging people to bring their plans, suggestions and ideas forward and you're sharing your views too, but ultimately you're trusting your team members to do what's necessary and to own the decisions they make, within their sphere of influence. This accountability may feel liberating for some, daunting for others; if people have been conditioned to a more directive or rule-based way of working, they can find this shift to a trust-based approach uncomfortable initially.

Establishing *accountability* is also about how you recognize excellent contributions and deal with under-performance. Holding people to a certain bar, not out of fear but through your shared purpose and pride in high standards, can be inspiring. It requires regular and robust performance management conversations, something many organizations find difficult to achieve consistently and even harder in diverse organizations where there may be more reticence around honest appraisals. Leaders I've spoken to acknowledge that when colleagues don't meet the bar, sometimes it's the individual's fault, sometimes it's the company's fault for not being clear enough and more often it's a bit of both.

Finally, a strong sense of *accountability* emerges from the way you approach experimentation, risk, and failure. If you're giving people freedom within your 'red lines' to figure out how to achieve objectives, then *they* decide the right next step to take. If they fail, that's not under-performing; it's collective learning. By sharing both positive and negative outcomes openly and without blame you can build confidence in innovating and problem-solving while strengthening diversity of thought and psychological safety. Early-stage start-ups offer a valuable reminder here to use experimentation, as a way to identify, as quickly as possible, which efforts are value-creating and which are wasteful; in *The Lean Start-up*, Eric Ries calls this 'validated learning'. Similarly applying psychologist Dr Carol Dweck's growth mindset philosophy[2] encourages people to view setbacks and disappointing outcomes as learning opportunities rather than failure and to persist with difficult challenges.

Programmes

The freedom framework's second aspect is your people programmes and how these build *capability* and *connection* across your organization, to give employees opportunities to grow and to encourage interpersonal and inter-team social bonds.

Building capability

This is about how you develop people's skills and careers, nurture future leaders and deep technical experts, resource people onto work and move them around your organization as the needs and opportunities evolve. In HR programme terms, it's learning and development, career development, talent management, mobility, resourcing, sponsorship, coaching, mentoring, rewards, and recognition. The other crucial ingredient in building capability is having good people managers; Chapter 14 looks specifically at developing managers' skills and confidence to lead their teams in today's (and tomorrow's) complex and shifting work environment.

First, be fully transparent about what people can expect. Are you offering something very structured or more fluid? Is it a 50/50 partnership between employee and employer, or up to the individual to make happen? At one international banking and wealth management group, colleagues are encouraged to curate their own careers rather than follow linear career paths and responsibility is assigned based on the type of work you do rather than your job title. In another organization, people wanted to be shown very clearly what their possible career paths and timelines looked like. Rewards require transparency too: despite a temptingly higher-paid offer elsewhere, a valued employee will often choose to stay if they can see how their rewards will progress in line with their career – it isn't always about 'more money now'. By carefully managing expectations and then implementing impactful programmes, you're creating strong glue that ties people to your organization, meeting your needs and theirs.

Capability building starts early, before a new employee even enters the workforce. Organizations are investing in skills programmes in schools to build students' self-belief, communication skills, and work readiness, recognizing that these vary enormously depending on the social background and education route of the individual. The pay-off to the employer is a more consistent level of confidence and capability in front of clients.

The best way to build capability is to create opportunities through growth. Split out a burgeoning team into two and create new career tracks around innovative areas of work. The law firm Ashurst has created a flexible 'Advance Delivery' programme setting out potential career options in the emerging field of 'new law' and the skills and attributes required in different roles.

Don't just rely on traditional 'vertical' career ladders and assume that will suffice for your business or your employees: not everyone is destined to manage large teams or P&Ls. Look as well at 'horizontal' development routes that recognize and draw out other strengths and motivations your people have. In doing so, you'll cultivate recognized experts in different fields who will generate just as much value – in terms of innovation, thought-leadership, and brand power – for your business as for your vertical career ladder climbers. You saw in Chapter 8 how internal job markets enable talent matching under certain conditions and put more agency into employees' hands, for example, consulting firm PwC's My+ platform allows people to choose what type of work they do, with whom, where, and how much they travel. If you can't justify an AI-powered investment yet, then an effective tech-light approach is to appoint a career champion (separate to the line manager) for every employee, who supports their advancement during their tenure.

Many organizations have talent management models and processes to identify high potential individuals but talent discussions risk being hollow words with little impact unless you can translate your conclusions into concrete next steps and activities for individuals to take advantage of. What are the specific development experiences that people need? How are you measuring the impact of these over the next six to 12 months? Ensure your talent programmes are action-oriented and you know what outcomes you're seeing as a result.

Sparking connection

Resourcing is often an under-optimized lever, but when you make creative, even bold, resourcing decisions you can simultaneously multiply and solidify cross-workforce connections. Make full use of short-term project inputs, job rotations, longer-term swaps and secondments and temporary promotions to cover absences, and consider appointing dedicated resourcing managers to support this. Look beyond your business's boundaries too: one CEO I know has piloted an industry-wide programme for middle managers in financial services to rotate around different organizations, broaden their skills and expand their network, with a 'no poaching' rule until the programme concludes.

Role hierarchies, office design, and narrow filters all act as unhelpful barriers to connection. Organizations that excel at fostering connection facilitate direct access for younger colleagues to senior executives for career chats, organize informal career talks and 'lunch and learns' and bring in expert speakers from adjacent or unrelated fields. They expose people to broader thinking while enabling them to establish contacts beyond their immediate team or cohort.

These conversations shouldn't always be work-related; in Chapter 1, we heard from Professor Robin Dunbar on the value of social time. 'Providing opportunities to build relationships through casual social interaction is probably the most important thing a senior leader can do', asserts Robin, 'because it pays dividends in a way unlike anything else'.[3] Work drinks, eating together, singing together, knitting clubs, running clubs, treasure hunts, you name it – these all fortify connection in measurably valuable ways.

Finally, design connection into your DNA by investing in intentional relationship building to reduce silos and disengagement. Train leaders in empathic listening and truthful talking and you will see this investment ripple out far and wide because when people start to see others, particularly influential colleagues or colleagues whom they respect, remove their social mask, they feel more prepared to follow suit. Measurement has proven this increases wellbeing, belonging, innovation, and retention.

Practices

The third aspect of the freedom framework is 'the way you do things around here': your everyday organizational habits, or norms. Every leader I've spoken to has commented on the fundamental importance of building *trust* and *transparency*; these twin tenets create a strong backbone that permits your organization to operate with freedom. They work as a double loop with one reinforcing the other: by being transparent you encourage trust to grow and when you trust people more, you're more confident about being more transparent with them.

'The way we do things around here' is manifested in observable behaviours and use of language, and also what *isn't* commonly done or spoken about. Over time, these factors reinforce a value system, a set of deep, shared beliefs about what matters here and what it takes to succeed around here. Robin Dunbar's research shows that trust operates most naturally within a 'tribe' of around 150 people who share similar values; in bigger organizations, multiple tribes may exist. The key is to keep asking yourself: what does trusting your employees look like in practice? What decisions and actions will confirm to people that you trust them? Particularly during tough times because these are especially revealing.

Here are seven practices that help to build trust and transparency:

1. Sharing more than you are comfortable with

Whether it's the raw, unvarnished financial picture or a half-formed idea, people respond positively to openness. Nervousness about operating beyond a 'need to know' basis is understandable, but as General Stanley McChrystal says in *Team of Teams*, in order to create a 'shared consciousness' people have to understand the whole system. One professional I spoke to recalled how their employer's regular 'warts and all' all-staff updates galvanized everyone to hit their ambitious targets. In written communications, don't hide behind the anonymous 'we' – own your message transparently and make it clear who it is coming from. It's the same principle as trust between buyers and sellers: my husband and I give a wide berth to faceless online retailers or service providers who avoid providing a phone number, address, or names of leaders. You can also increase the transparency of your governance mechanisms by opening up executive meetings to selected colleagues via rotating (temporary) places at the table; setting up NextCos, fixed-term teams of junior or mid-career colleagues who debate the executive team's agenda items and propose recommendations; and establishing mirror boards that shadow your appointed Board.

2. Addressing unfairness

In any organization there's often a gap between what is espoused and what *actually* happens. This is partly caused by biased processes that unintentionally advantage some and disadvantage others and by in-groups and out-groups forming around power and access; it's also about opaque rules that aren't openly disclosed. If you don't know what these implicit or hidden rules are, you're at a disadvantage. In employee focus groups I've conducted over the years, a recurring frustration that people cite is a lack of transparency surrounding how people get selected for work opportunities, talent programmes, and promotions.

So, as leaders, it's essential to review your people data forensically to see who's over- and under-represented at different levels, in your talent programmes and pipeline and in terms of tenure in role, to identify groups or individuals who are being repeatedly overlooked. In parallel, continuously test your people processes – and your own assumptions and world views – for bias by seeking out the perspectives and experiences of others through listening sessions, leaver research, and stay interviews; these will hold the mirror up to reflect how inclusive and visible opportunities and work policies, such as around flexibility, are in practice.

3. Respecting people's expertise

In the next chapter, I'll look at expectations of leaders' expertise but an important glue-building practice is to acknowledge when you don't have all the answers and to work on developing these together, or better still, trusting in others' skills and experience. There is nothing more frustrating to capable professionals than being hired for their expertise only to be excluded from relevant conversations and decisions or for their recommendations to be ignored. Unfortunately, we're wired to dive in with our own opinions: our innate righting reflex drives our desire to solve problems and a cognitive bias known as the Dunning–Kruger effect means we typically overestimate our abilities in domains in which we have limited competence; amusingly, the first rule of the Dunning–Kruger club is you don't know you're a member.[4] But according to organizational psychologist and Professor Adam Grant in his book *Think Again*, 'when experts express doubt they become more persuasive' so by freely admitting what you don't know, you are building followership through your transparency.

4. Letting others take decisions

In *Team of Teams*, General McChrystal advocates for 'empowered execution' where leaders are 'eyes on, hands off'. Organizations with high levels of People Glue decentralize decision-making as much as possible: they trust colleagues to work autonomously, involve the right people and ask for help when they need it. Timpsons, the British chain of watch repair and key cutting service shops, attributes its success to its 'upside-down management' that gives employees full freedom to serve customers. They famously have only two rules: 'look the part' and 'put the money in the till', and as you walk in the door, a sign informs you that the manager has authority to make the decisions they think are right for the customer.

One client I worked with provides another example of empowered execution: the CEO and COO engaged me to run workshops with all 25 of their teams over the course of a year to equip their people with the confidence and skills to identify changes *within their control* that would help them deliver better for clients, work smarter not harder, and further strengthen their collaborative culture. Their explicit message to colleagues was 'we trust you to figure out the answers and to take action yourselves'.

Applying this practice to the return-to-office vs hybrid-working debate, top-down mandates rarely work effectively: much better are broad organizational guidelines with each team working out locally how to apply these in practice. For example, one national bank expects employees to spend 40% of their time each month in the office but rather than specify how many days per week, they've guided people on the types of work that are best done in-person in the office and the types of work that are best suited to remote-working, and left teams to figure out the rest. Organizations adopting this approach are seeing attrition come down, talent attraction and productivity go up.

5. Welcoming healthy debates

Building People Glue isn't about prioritizing niceness and agreeing all the time but about being able to express differences in opinions constructively and respectfully. Highly successful cultures are not always light-hearted happy places but where people are energized but focused on solving hard problems together. There is a difference between relationship conflict and task conflict; by tending carefully to relationships, it becomes easier to manage task conflict and performance is less likely to be jeopardized. Healthy debates require people to give and receive honest feedback but as Adam Grant says, 'it's surprisingly easy to hear a hard truth when it comes from someone who believes in your potential and cares about your success'. The same applies for performance feedback which I'll cover more in Chapter 14.

6. Unpacking communications

When the adult-to-adult transactional discussion (see Chapter 4) regresses to an adult-to-child conversation, frustrations and grievances mount and the proportion of people who leave because of a breakdown in communication is high. So how are you engaging people in adult-adult discussions and how well-equipped are your managers to do the same with their teams? To communicate carefully and effectively we need to be aware of our own filters and assumptions: Chris Argyris' 'ladder of inference' is a helpful tool for unpacking unspoken assumptions in conversations in a way that leads to better outcomes. Generally, by making the effort to share your underlying thinking, acknowledge your own emotions and your levels of confidence or uncertainty, you build trust and bring people with you. Be mindful of your choice of words and labels, because language isn't a passive or neutral medium but an active medium that indicates the things we value and don't value.

7. Backing people's potential

I've lost count of the number of times senior leaders guesting on my podcast have pointed to a particular career moment when someone senior nudged them to consider a stretching opportunity or a promotion they felt to be out of reach. All acknowledged the powerful impact of someone else trusting their potential and acting on this. Ways you can practice this regularly in your organization include moving people before they are ready, inviting them to lead parts of big set-piece events, and establishing a formal sponsorship programme. Unlike mentoring, which focuses predominantly on one-way sharing of experience, sponsorship is a public two-way reciprocal relationship in which both parties' benefit. It is a manifestation of trust where the senior leader is willing to share their social and reputation capital for a more junior colleague.

Advice for leaders

Your business metrics, workforce data, and employee research should offer a guide to how well you're establishing alignment and accountability, capability and connection, trust and transparency; here are some complementary methods:

Parameters: notice the 'red flags', i.e. the signs that your parameters may need reinforcing or adjusting. There are two kinds of red flags:

- First, signals alerting you that certain colleagues or teams are close to transgressing your operating tramlines. Sometimes this is for positive reasons: when people are being truly innovative, they tend to be operating 'near the edge'. Other times, this may be mavericks insisting on doing things their own way and in need of reining in.
- Second, indicators – such as short tenures, people bringing problems not solutions, a reluctance to volunteer – that your organizational controls are boxing people in, limiting their freedom to operate and disempowering them in their day jobs.

Programmes: Be selective with your investment of money, time, and effort and keep measuring the outcomes that these are achieving.

- With capability-building, look at the longer-term results such as people securing promotions or lateral moves, talent pipelines diversifying and even valued employees leaving for bigger roles elsewhere (they may boomerang back).
- With connection-building, include questions on social connectedness and loneliness in your employee survey (see Gallup and Meta's 2023 global report for ideas[5]). Conduct an organizational network analysis for a visual representation of how people and teams interact, where your influential 'bridging' employees are located and any gaps in connection.

Practices: Borrow from anthropologists who read social and cultural contexts as outsiders looking in:

- Hard as it is to remove our insider 'goggles', try to look with fresh eyes at your organizational environment and habits. What attitudes, language and behaviour do you observe? What might you be overlooking because your practices are so familiar? Tune into the social silences* and what may be hiding in plain sight.

- Invite recent joiners to share what *they've* noticed, asking them what's different to where they worked before or to their pre-joining expectations. Talk to leavers too (only voluntary leavers) by conducting qualitative and quantitative leaver research. By talking to both joiners and leavers, you'll likely uncover a fuller truth than is revealed from exit interviews only.

Advice for individuals

Looking back at your time so far with your current organization (or your last role if you are between jobs right now) what is it about their:

- *Parameters* that gives you freedom to operate?
- *Programmes* that helps you grow professionally?
- *Practices* that encourages you to be your authentic self at work?

Note down a few observations, aiming to be as specific as possible. These reflections may help you understand better what's motivating you to stay with your employer for the time being, or for the longer-term and what you may risk sacrificing if you move elsewhere.

If your answers are less positive because you're feeling dissatisfied with the status quo, then use your reflections to identify what

---

* Topics, issues, or behaviours that are present but not openly discussed.

you're missing. What actions can you take or conversations can you initiate to improve your experience of work and opportunities right now? If you've already concluded it's time to move on, then focus any exploratory recruitment conversations on the parameters, programmes and practices that are most important to you, to maximize your chances of a more fulfilling outcome in your next organization.

No rolling back

If you're a leader, I hope this chapter's freedom framework helps you to strike a successful balance in your organization between Aldous Huxley's total anarchy, and total efficiency. But what happens if and when freedom falters? In the next chapter, I'll set out how you can manage the risks of letting go and still maintain momentum in the face of setbacks.

Chapter 12
When freedom falters

'No plan survives first contact with the enemy'.

Helmuth von Moltke the Elder

The best-laid plans

IF YOU'RE A leader reading this, you might fall into one of two categories: the action-oriented enthusiast who has already decided 'we absolutely need this now, let's dive in' or the cautious pragmatist who's thinking 'this could transform our business, but it could also go badly wrong'. Neither stance is wrong, but it definitely pays to recognize there may be pitfalls as you progress: even the best-laid plans can look vulnerable when faced with the unpredictability of real-world situations.

Creating People Glue by offering more freedom is not risk-free and it may not work perfectly for your organization at first; in fact, you will likely encounter some challenges as you shift your modus operandi and loosen the controls. Formula One racing legend, Lewis Hamilton, said after his first, highly anticipated drive for Ferrari in early 2025 where he placed 10th, 'it's not how you fought, it how's you get back up'; similarly in your transition to greater organizational freedom what matters is how you deal with any setbacks. So, in this chapter I explain how to diagnose the issue that has arisen and how to respond in a way that strengthens your organizational freedom instead of undermining it.

Teething problems

So, how high risk is the move to offer greater freedom? It partly depends on your organization and your state of readiness. In larger organizations there are often so many priorities and teams that it's harder to align everyone around your common goal and the chance that your critical messages get distorted is high. In smaller organizations, it's slightly easier to get everyone lined up and pointing in the same direction, metaphorically speaking. In terms of readiness, if you've already done some of the groundwork described in Chapter 11 of establishing parameters, programmes, and practices, you'll be better placed to mitigate the likelihood and impact of any bumps along the way. Even if your culture already oozes freedom, mismatches of expectations can still give you an uncomfortable nip, for example, when new joiners mistakenly interpret a high-freedom environment as being laid back and leisurely. And freedom isn't fixed forever: as your industry drivers, competitors, and talent pools change so your approach to freedom will need to keep evolving however successfully you've managed it to date.

So, what are examples of freedom faltering? With the four freedoms of Part 3 in mind, it may manifest as people exceeding their authority in deal-making or expenditure; working questionable hours with extended office absences; previously good performance nose-diving or someone's promising career trajectory stalling; unmoderated self-expression morphing into disrespectful or discriminatory language or behaviour; presenteeism or quiet quitting replacing energized, value-adding work.

Setbacks serve a useful purpose: they motivate you to keep monitoring your organizational checks and balances and course-correcting. As parenting expert Anita Cleare reminds us:

> Accountability and boundaries often don't get met for very good reasons. The point of a boundary is not about guaranteeing safety or instant success, but about structuring learning.

By adopting a growth mindset in dealing with setbacks, your leadership team and organization will grow in confidence in managing freedom and reap the rewards. As one CEO commented:

> Yes, there are times when freedom comes back to bite us but I would take it all day, every day because the benefits of the bigger picture far outweigh the small risks along the way.

Diagnose before ditching

Unintended consequences of offering more freedom may be concerning, even potentially deleterious and a natural reflex reaction is to ratchet up your controls by increasing governance, managing more tightly, reducing local decision-making. However, it is critical to avoid overreacting. When you overreact, the rest of the organization interprets your response as evidence that you'd never genuinely believed in that freedom in the first place and *this interpretation* is what breaches employer-employee trust and damages workforce relations.

Equally, searching for someone to blame is a short-sighted strategy: finger-pointing drives fear and disempowerment which discourages people from speaking up, being proactive or taking responsibility for decisions. In time this reduces your organization's agility and creativity; William McKnight, the President and later Chair of 3M who we met in Chapter 11, warned that 'management that is destructively critical when mistakes are made kills initiative'.[1]

Following an unwanted consequence of freedom, take care not to apply unnecessary additional guardrails as these will constrain people's autonomy, growth, self-expression, and their ability to do meaningful work. While those involved in the breach may need to prove they can operate successfully *within* the parameters and practices you've established, resist the urge to restrict freedom for broader groups. As a company you've got to commit to a single way of working, even if there are team-by-team nuances depending on the function or service they provide.

When a freedom is reduced or withdrawn, people often discover it is more important to them than they had previously appreciated and its retraction prompts them to re-evaluate their role and commitment to their organization. An obvious example of this is the rolling-back of work flexibility and the enforcing of in-office attendance four or five days a week by employers, which we saw ensue in late 2024 and 2025 in certain sectors like financial services and technology. When handled badly, organizations found that innovation, inter-team collaboration, and work culture plummeted, their best performers and more diverse talent were the first to leave, and it was harder to attract and hire replacements.[2]

However the challenge or setback manifests, you'll need to understand why and how it occurred and crucially, to differentiate between different types of 'wrongs'. Look closely and honestly at the organization's role as well as at the employee's role and as leaders, ask yourselves whether you failed the individual or they failed you. When freedom falters, typically one of the following four scenarios are playing out:

1. A clear *transgression* by the individual of your modus operandi.
2. A *mutual mistake* from which you can both draw valuable learning.
3. *Inadequate performance* by the employee.
4. An employee *overstaying* in terms of tenure.

Let's look at each of these in turn.

Transgressions

This is where the employee has breached their employment contract or psychological contract* either wilfully or through negligence despite the employer being unequivocally clear about what is expected and permitted and what's not. The cause may vary – it could result from resistance to new proposals, decisions, or organizational changes that the individual cannot commit to; it can be a cultural mistake that has crept up more invisibly; or it can be due to the individual(s) seeking a different kind of freedom to the version you're offering.

With deliberate wilfulness, negligence, or a cavalier or maverick attitude, direct feedback is required to spell out the issue and the consequences; potentially even disciplinary action. In some ways the more problematic cause is the cultural mistake, because of the potential for seemingly minor or isolated 'under the radar' transgressions to evolve into more widespread activity with deeper ramifications. A salient example is the unregulated use of WhatsApp and other private (and unrecorded) messaging tools in regulated industries such as banking and finance, where certain work conversations are required to take place on recorded phone lines. While every bank will undoubtedly have an e-comms policy, this hasn't prevented widescale misuse of private messaging tools at all organizational levels, resulting in billions of fines across the banking sector. Clearly people know that it is not the right thing to do, but they stop feeling bad because they know everyone else is doing it.

So, how do you mitigate transgressions of this nature? First, by making it safe for people to speak up so that dissent and opposing views have a healthy outlet; if they've had the chance to challenge and make their views known, people are less likely to rebel. Second, make it crystal clear what people are being held accountable for and lay out the consequences in advance. Third, confront the difficult decisions that may need to be taken. As leaders you will need to

* The unwritten and informal set of expectations between employer and employee.

ascertain whether individuals are still aligned to what you're trying to achieve and how you are going about it. It may become inevitable that someone has reached their career ceiling with you, that others are promoted over them or even that the individual's chapter with your organization comes to an end.

Mutual mistakes

This second scenario is where the employee has made an unwise decision or acted inappropriately but it becomes clear that the organization was also partly to blame. Perhaps operating guidelines were ambiguous, work had not been clearly commissioned or delegated, or a manager had failed to communicate clearly in other ways with the individual. It's important to consider the full facts and the broader culture within which this scenario unfolded, for example any oversights, pressures, or circumstances that led to the employees behaving as they did. Mutual mistakes provide as much of a learning opportunity for managers and leaders as they do for team members.

With the best will in the world, genuine mistakes will happen every now and again. I still wince at certain *faux pas* I made earlier in my career, including emailing my project plan for my first ever property purchase to our client (an Executive team member no less) instead of the project plan for the transformation we were supporting them on, and accidentally omitting some slides from a high-profile event for the top 150 leaders at a client organization, leaving the poor speaker to *ad lib* from memory (he was unforgettably kind to me about it afterwards). I can't claim these mistakes were anyone's fault but my own, but a bit less project haste and a bit more rigour in reviewing work outputs would have undoubtedly helped.

Those organizations that have freedom in their DNA have a deliberate approach to mutual mistakes. They recognize that failures help people to learn what to do differently next time, that they open a door to growth. They aim to normalize failure, and to see it as an integral element of doing great work by talking about what's gone wrong and what people have learnt as a result. In doing so, they're building a healthy dynamic where colleagues are encouraged to share honestly, get thoughtful about mistakes, and bring ideas for better ways of working or solutions. This builds trust and collaboration; as one CEO of a high-growth company said to me 'we failed so many times but the team stuck together'. That's not to say mistakes are plain sailing – sometimes people need extra support for a while if they're finding a new role particularly stretching or their confidence is knocked by the setback.

Inadequate performance

This third scenario relates to managerial capability: an inability or a reluctance to deal with an employee who is underperforming. Whether they are simply doing the bare minimum, hiding in the middle of the herd or deploying diversion tactics like ostentatious presenteeism or behavioural busyness while achieving very little, ultimately tolerating this underperformance drags down the team as a whole and undermines the freedoms you're offering. There is little that frustrates people more than a team member not pulling their weight or being ill-equipped for their role and a manager failing to grip this issue firmly, to the extent that teams have been known to 'spit people out' and 'cut loafers loose'.

Not gripping poor performance is short-sighted from a commercial and financial perspective because you don't just want people to stay, you want their drive, their passion, and their discretionary effort – your business momentum and success depends on this. Tolerating underperformance is equivalent to having a hugely powerful battery that you're not recharging. It can also bring the added sting of causing your brightest talent to look elsewhere.

Good managers skilled at managing performance strike a balance between treating people as individuals and maintaining fairness across the board. Before jumping to conclusions or taking action, they have open conversations with the employee to find out what may be going on, what they are finding hard and why. Are they experiencing barriers at work that are discouraging them? Is something significant going on in their home life? They enquire, empathize, and listen well. They also bring evidence in the form of objective data into the conversation and don't shy away from difficult feedback. Sometimes this adept intervention opens up new possibilities such as a move into a less pressurized role or one more suited to the individual's strengths, and it's hugely rewarding to see that individual start to flourish and soar following a well-considered decision. Sometimes the opposite outcome is unavoidable too, when you have to make a judgement call about someone who simply isn't thriving in your organization.

Overstaying

For this final scenario, recall the golden triangle in Chapter 2 where we saw how the trifecta of good pay, interesting work and flexibility persuades people to stay. The flipside of the golden triangle is that it can cause people to get too comfortable and to stay *too long*. Someone in this situation might muse: 'I have freedom, I can work from home, I enjoy my work, and I'm reasonably well paid'. They become a comfortable coaster lacking a burning platform to progress or to leave, who decides to sit tight and watch the months or years slide by particularly when the wider economic context is unfavourable. The glue works for them, but not for your business.

In organizations where the reward policy is to pay top quartile salaries or where you have long-tenure employees whose salaries have met or exceeded the ceiling for their expertise, pay acts as a golden handcuff pricing people out of the market. Flexibility of working arrangements can similarly make people reluctant to move on for fear of being forced to accept reduced flexibility elsewhere, particularly if the individual has a long commute, caring responsibilities, is neurodiverse, has health conditions, or disabilities. And anyone who has done a long stint at one organization will recognize how much they've invested in their personal network and internal brand over the years and how daunting the prospect of starting over again at a new company is. Neuroscientists have ascertained that we value the status quo more than the unknown because of the cost we associate with change and the fear of loss.

Sometimes, it's simply a reverse case of 'I did what I came to do', i.e., despite having been a valued contributor in the past, the employee no longer offers what the employer is seeking for the future. As business needs change, so certain skills, ambitions, and motivations come to the fore while others recede and it may be time to have an honest and mutually respectful conversation about a parting of ways.

Advice for leaders

Which of the above four scenarios have you observed most/ least in your organization and what hypotheses might you draw from this?

How do you and other leaders typically respond when things go wrong?

- Do you reach for quick fixes like reshuffling roles and responsibilities, appointing a senior person to get more closely involved, or request more frequent or detailed update reports?
- Or do you call the relevant people together to reflect in a non-judgmental way on what went wrong and what they – and you – might do differently next time?

How effective are your performance management processes and conversations: are underperformers coasting under the radar or are they being managed attentively with a clear messaging, appropriate support and failing that, material consequences? If it's the former, what's causing or enabling this to happen?

Which are the hardest conversations you might need to have with potential overstayers? How can you thoughtfully open up a dialogue with them to see where they are at and how they're viewing the future? It's tempting and understandable to want to kick such a conversation into the long grass or hope the situation will naturally resolve itself, but it's also possible the individuals concerned are silently wrestling with the same question and feel relieved that you're raising it.

If you're planning ways to encourage greater freedom – autonomy, growth, self-expression, meaningful work, or other – try conducting a pre-mortem with the leadership team or a cross-section of colleagues. What could potentially go wrong and what different ways could you respond?

Advice for individuals

Think back to a recent time when you experienced a setback at work. To avoid natural defensiveness, imagine you're an outsider looking in.

- What did you get wrong?
- What could you have done differently?
- What didn't you get from others that could have resulted in a better outcome?
- What will you pay greater attention to next time?

How do you react to perceived failure? Do you:

- Blame yourself, blame others, or both?
- Double down on reducing risk by playing it safer or protecting your own back?
- Look dispassionately at what happened and invite others' views?

The latter is arguably harder to do and requires humility but is more transformational.

If you've received negative feedback about your performance recently, what do you (honestly) attribute this to: a lack of skill? Confidence? Motivation? Clarity? Home distractions or worries spilling over into work? We can be surprisingly resourceful at developing coping strategies that deter us from resolving the underlying issues. Talk to someone you trust, inside or outside the organization, about what's going on and what would help you raise your game.

If you suspect you're in the 'overstaying' category, try asking people you trust how they knew when it was time to leave a job they'd enjoyed and been effective in. Did they leave at the right time, too early, or too late and why? (The most common decision is 'too late'.) What advice can they offer?

Adapt and evolve

To summarize this chapter's advice on how to respond when freedom falters: avoid knee-jerk reactions, gather reliable data, and make proportional, evidence-based decisions without unnecessary prevarication or delay. Accept, in the best growth-mindset way, that there's probably some learning for everyone to take from any setbacks you experience as you loosen the reins and foster greater freedom at work. Failure might never feel fun but you can work to make it less frightening for people and even something familiar and helpful that walks companionably alongside success. And that experience and environment becomes, in itself, a powerful motivator for people to stay.

But what about you personally? Leaders today are faced with limitless demands on their time and a burden of impossible expectations, from navigating the organization safely through turbulent times to demonstrating moral and social responsibility on issues unfolding far beyond their operating footprint. When it comes to leading freedom, what do leaders today want and need?

Chapter 13
Leading freedom

'The wise man does not lay up his own treasures. The more he gives to others, the more he has for his own.'

Lao Tzu

Growing glue

THIS CHAPTER IS not about 'how to lead' in a general sense; there is a vast quantity of advice on leadership skills in the form of books, talks, other resources, and consultancy by respected executives, leadership advisors, armed forces leaders, organizational psychologists, elite sportspeople, and more. Here, we're looking very specifically at *what is required of you as a leader* in offering greater freedom to your employees to strengthen retention.

In contrast to Chapter 11 which provides a practical organizational framework for operationalizing freedom, this chapter sets out the role you as a leader can play in fostering an environment of greater freedom. It acknowledges the personal risks, dilemmas, and vulnerabilities that you may experience in doing so and that you may personally desire and benefit from freedom too. It proposes how you might best direct your own time and energies, and it explores the significant part that self-awareness plays, including of your own past experiences of power and freedom, and how appropriate support from others is essential.

All things to all people, everywhere

In the Introduction we heard the view that 'there's never been as much thrown at a CEO as there is right now'. Gone are those leisurely days when organizations focused on one strategic initiative at time, paused to let the dust settle then started to consider the next. Today, uncertainty and change are multi-layered constants, combining major top-down programmatic change and smaller technological or process updates that still require people to relinquish established habits and learn new ones. Leaders are orchestrating multiple changes that place heavy demands on operating bandwidth and resilience and risk leaving people buffeted by confusion and complexity. Leaders are also feeling the impact of these upheavals on themselves, learning new approaches, operating outside their comfort zones and expending huge effort and energy in their role.

At the same time, workers and the media increasingly tend to judge an entire organization by whether they approve or disapprove of a key policy or decision, by the organization's stance on broader social matters, by the leaders' own personal political or social views and even by the circles they associate with outside of work. Leaders are increasingly being looked at to be the flag carriers of everything good – they're being asked to be not just 'vertical' leaders in the traditional sense, but 'horizontal' enterprise leaders across all these issues; but they haven't been trained to be the latter. The court of public opinion can hem executives in by holding them to vertiginous, even impossible standards then reject them swiftly when they fall short. In Chapter 6, we noted the steady global decline in trust in authority figures; only 53% of people say they trust CEOs in general, with a higher proportion (67%) saying they trust their *own* CEO – but not as much as they trust scientists and teachers.[1] Little wonder then that many CEOs feel compelled to tread extremely carefully and admit to an inner insecurity, reluctant to share their true views publicly for fear of isolating or antagonizing employees, clients, or shareholders. For many leaders in today's environment, that is like career kryptonite'.* Other leaders have shared that they feel vulnerable if they speak up and they word their responses cautiously out of fear of being personally attacked. So, for those in positions of power, psychological safety – and indeed, physical safety† – is not guaranteed and often feels unattainable.

Leaders also face the challenge of having to satisfy investor or shareholder expectations to both 'perform and transform', to have a firm grip on the 'here and now' while also actively planning for one to two years out. CEOs tell me that their business plans are about managing the twin tracks of daily product or service delivery and audacious 'moonshots' that will shape the business and its success in the years to come. Robust, resilient, and foresighted strategies are required, and alongside these rational and logical elements so too is maturity and skill in managing the emotional and relational aspects of change and uncertainty, in order to bring people with them and coax out their discretionary effort.

In the midst of these complex challenges, leaders need freedom too. Many are consciously contracting to secure the freedom to develop their organization, or part of it, within the broader framework they have signed up to. A CEO of a major international joint venture told me he needed clarity on what he was accountable for delivering and for his boss to hold him to that, but equally he needed the freedom to get on with delivering in his own way and support for his plans and decisions, while accepting some challenge and pushback on certain actions. This is echoed by other leaders: having freedom to *grow* a business and not just manage the margins; having the autonomy to determine

---

* Kryptonite is a fictional poisonous material that appears in the Superman stories; it weakens his superpowers and is potentially lethal. So, career kryptonite means a career-damaging or career-ending scenario or action.
† Brian Thompson, the CEO of US health insurance company UnitedHealthcare, was fatally shot on the streets of Manhattan in December 2024 by a 26-year-old man angry about insurance companies' refusals to pay out certain claims.

the priorities and set out their own agenda, not just chasing other people's agendas; and having a 'seat at the table' when appropriate.

Letting go

In cultivating a high-freedom environment to better retain employees, the most critical decision you can take as a leader is to relinquish a culture of command and control. Instead, focus on setting a clear direction, commissioning work, holding people accountable for delivering, and continuously tuning in to assess how you're doing. You're concentrating on the 'what' and the 'how', where the 'what' is setting the strategic direction and having daily conversations at the front line of delivery and the 'how' is defining the cultural umbrella, the way in which you expect people to operate. Where there are blockers and bottlenecks, step in to resolve these so people can deliver unimpeded, but otherwise, step back and let people get on with things within the parameters and practices you have established.

Our instinct is to hold on, for reasons that run deep within us, because we all have underlying basic human needs that unconsciously drive our actions and interactions. A need for recognition or competence could drive a reluctance to let others outshine us and competitive rather than collaborative behaviour; a need for control or perfectionism could reduce our trust in others to deliver exactly as we would and lead us to micro-manage or intervene unnecessarily, squashing people's confidence and agency. Micromanaging cascades unproductively down the organization so that people end up scared to do anything and the leader persecuted by their job. As psychoanalyst Ernest Schachtel explained, 'letting go of every kind of clinging opens the fullest view... but it is this very letting go which often arouses the greatest amount of anxiety'. Every new situation represents a 'little dying' of an aspect of our identity or world view that we've previously clung to,[2] consequently our response is to grip ever tighter.

One example of letting go is to fight the urge to always provide the answer or find the fastest, easiest route to obtaining this. Instead, recognize that we are all hampered by filters, blindspots, and biased decisions, so invite challenge and opposing views. Give people explicit permission to ask any question and to sense-make collaboratively. There's an inevitable tension involved here: in certain circumstances, co-creating an approach or outcome may be highly advantageous because it will result in a better-quality solution and secure people's buy-in. But co-creating takes longer because you're dealing with a plurality of views and brokering a consensus, and it can in parallel throw up some uncomfortable realities that need to be addressed. So sometimes we shirk away from co-creating and take the seemingly quicker path (which doesn't necessarily lead to the best outcomes later).

Another example is rejecting the primacy of technical expertise or cognitive intelligence and accepting that social and emotional intelligence are equally vital. Social intelligence is our ability to 'read' and navigate social interactions, while emotional intelligence is our ability to recognize and manage emotions in ourselves and others. Organizational change efforts notoriously fail when leaders pay insufficient attention to the relational and emotional aspects of change, leaving people resisting new ways of working. If you're thinking 'but as leader I need to project confidence and certainty', yes at times this is undoubtedly called for. But there are other moments when you can share your doubts or vulnerability and in doing so, build trust and followership.

Letting go will likely require you to invest in a shift in the performance and capability of your leadership team. If used to an exclusively operational focus, you'll need to broaden your outlook to engage in more strategic debates. If you've previously viewed the organization as a set of mechanical levers to push or pull, you'll need to recognize social dynamics and how the way you 'show up' everyday impacts and influences others. If you believe you can mandate behaviour change via top-down transformation projects or three-line whips,‡ you'll benefit from learning how you can

‡ A three-line whip is an instruction issued to British Members of Parliament to vote a certain way in accordance with their party's official stance or face potential expulsion from the party.

encourage meaningful change through exploratory conversations. When you invest more time and energy in practising enquiry, active listening, and empathy, and in coaching direct reports to do the same, you'll be rewarded with valuable feedback loops and an unleashing of people's discretionary effort and potential.

Know thyself

If you consider yourself a pretty enlightened being, I've got bad news. Only 15% of us are adequately self-aware, with a typical mismatch between our *self-perceived* vs *actual* competence of over 70%. A leader's lack of self-awareness negatively impacts decision-making, collaboration, and conflict management, and ditto for teams.[3] Many leaders hold onto an illusion of control, creating mechanisms to manage their anxieties that the things that they have initiated won't happen. By cultivating self-awareness through feedback, psychometric tools, reflection, and coaching, you can recognize these habitual thoughts and behaviours and consciously activate a different response.

We also gain by understanding our own preferences around freedom; you may feel more strongly about one or more of the four freedoms than others, for example. Parenting expert Anita Cleare, explains that as with parenting, our relationship with freedom is informed by our past, wider experiences of power, from how we were parented and taught, to what our first boss was like and what we've learnt from leaders we've admired. 'Everyone has their own inner working template of what leadership is' remarks Anita and this template determines the degree of freedom that we're comfortable offering. To become proficient in leading freedom, we have to be prepared to do the inner work involved because we'll inevitably be stepping outside of these comfort zones.

Yet organizations don't often allow the time and space for growing self- and other-awareness and it's not always seen as an essential capability to invest in. Consequently, executives carry around their own expectations of what it means to be a leader without admitting their uncertainties to anyone or comparing inner working templates. The consequence? Noticeably inconsistent patterns of response across a leadership team and clunky or clumsy conversations about emotions and behaviours. Coaching can help enormously yet it's often reserved for a minority of leaders or only introduced as a corrective measure following an 'issue' (e.g., formal complaints about an individual leader's behaviour).

Increasing self-awareness makes you as a leader more mentally and emotionally resilient when helping your organization to adapt to a high-freedom environment because you'll undoubtedly encounter resistance; Rick Maurer's model helpfully describes the three levels of change resistance as cognitive ('I don't get it'), emotional ('I don't like it'), and relational ('I don't like you').[4] Focusing exclusively on the rational plans for change (the cognitive part) is a recipe for failure; only by inviting people to share their emotional reactions to the change and consistently investing in building trust and transparency will you succeed in your efforts. With 'I don't like you', this doesn't mean you have to be nice all the time; indeed, I've heard several leaders say they have to 'fight their own niceness'. By not avoiding difficult conversations, by not misguidedly protecting people from uncomfortable realities or the anxiety of uncertainty, employees will recognize your strength and commitment to them as a leader, despite emotions running high.

Investing in self-awareness applies equally to the leadership team as a whole. Leading freedom requires you to share, debate, and act *as one*, to agree the behaviours to which you will hold yourselves accountable and to keep investing in this as the composition of the team and the business change. Your actions and responses as leaders are highly influential in shaping your organization's culture, including what you actively encourage, what you turn a blind eye to, and what you pick up on or constructively critique. All of these day-to-day interactions can grow or skew your culture in ways you may or may not anticipate or desire.

To successfully engender a high-freedom culture, you'll need to explore together questions such as: What does success look like for different stakeholders? For us personally? What strengths do we each bring and how might we get in our own way? An experienced coach and facilitator can help you appreciate the group dynamics at play in your leadership discussions, how diverse or otherwise you are as a team, your blindspots, reactions to conflict, and default stress responses. Over time, this builds a deeper shared understanding – a consistent working template – about what it means to be a leader in your organization and how you'll lead freedom effectively.

Team effort

While as leaders you need your own brand of freedom, your chances of success in leading freedom and creating glue are far higher when you are appropriately resourced. There's often pressure – from above or self-imposed – on leaders to prove themselves quickly but despite the relatively high failure rate when leaders transition into a new role, there's often a lack of robust support for leaders. Review and reassess what your onboarding looks like for external leadership appointments and what support is provided when colleagues are promoted internally or move internationally into senior roles. Make transition support for leaders the norm: this isn't about signalling or addressing weakness, it's about giving leaders the best chance of success right from day one so they can make an impact faster. If you're a leader stepping up or into a new role, then ask about transition support *before* you move. Examples of this include appointing a peer mentor and an external coach, access to networks of leaders in similar roles for confidential exchanges, focusing on early learning to close any confidence or capability gaps, and regular feedback and check-in conversations throughout your first year. And this isn't just for first-time leaders but for seasoned C-suite[¶] executives too; there is

---

[¶] This typically refers to the most senior level executives whose job titles include the term 'Chief' e.g., Chief Executive, Chief Technology Officer, Chief People Officer, etc.

an assumption that as leaders grow in experience and seniority, they can navigate their next role with ease, however, as they progress, the level of challenge and complexity increases and the support needs to keep pace with this.

We saw earlier how the whole leadership team needs to act collectively in leading freedom; in addition, certain functions play a valuable role too. HR can work closely with Finance to track robust data on turnover and associated costs, plus your employee research, people/HR analytics, and DEI professionals can collaborate to offer retention insights across functions, demographics (age, gender, race, disability, socio-economic background, etc.), and also manager capability. You should be able to drill down into the detailed picture of retention and identify the glue factors that are influencing the outcomes in each area.

Be mindful though that the HR and DEI functions aren't there to lead freedom on your behalf. As a Head of DEI in a multinational insurance company told me:

> We're like a travel agent – we can help leaders to consider their options, advise them on the best route, plan their trip and make sure they're ready to go but we can't take the journey for them.

Similarly, if you have an Organization Development team, their role is to help you as leader assess readiness, capacity, capability, resilience, and timing as you embark on cultivating freedom but they can't spearhead the effort or be solely accountable. They can hold the mirror up to help you perceive current practices more clearly and to reinforce your freedom framework with high-quality leadership and talent programmes, initiatives, and nudges to strengthen connection and inter-team glue, and to bridge silos.

Advice for leaders

Take some time to consider the following and where relevant ask others for their perspectives too:

Your own freedom

1. What past experiences of power, authority, control, and freedom have influenced you and how?
2. What feedback have you received that suggests you are more or less comfortable with offering the four freedoms described in Part 3?
3. Notice what has been curtailing your own freedom as a leader. Where or when do you feel most vulnerable? What is 'career kryptonite' for you?
4. What is your biggest fear around 'letting go'?
5. How might you renegotiate your implicit (or explicit) contract with whomever you report or answer to, to enhance your freedom to operate?

Freedom in your organization

6. On a scale of 1–10 (where 1 is not at all reliant, and 10 is extremely reliant), how reliant is your organization on 'command and control?'. Look at how decisions are made and by whom, how involved in the detail managers are, whether people bring problems or solutions, whether they wait for approval or act with agency.
7. What do you gain or lose by handing over more control to others within a clear framework? How might this shift the balance between your personal gain and your collective performance?
8. How might 'letting go' enable you to get the best out of your team?

Advice for individuals

What have you learnt from leaders and other authority figures you've encountered about holding on to control or letting go?

What underlying basic human needs might be influencing your interactions with others?[5]

How comfortable are you talking to your manager about the freedom you want or need to perform at your best and what you're getting or lacking right now? If it feels daunting, try the following four steps, using 'I' statements as much as possible:

1. Disclosure: e.g., 'I work best when I…'.
2. Feedback: e.g., 'I feel X when….'.
3. Proposal: e.g., 'Could we try Y differently?'.
4. Commitment: e.g., 'Like you, I want to see Z outcome for our team'.

Try broaching an informal conversation with colleagues about the four freedoms to discover what matters most to each of you and how your current experiences may be similar or different. Be prepared to share a reflection or two of your own first.

If you manage or mentor others, invite them to reflect on the four freedoms. Make sure you listen to understand rather than listen to respond, and acknowledge people's views in a non-judgmental way. A good outcome is for people to leave the conversation feeling heard so suppress any urge to dive in and fix a problem, which is 'rescuer' behaviour.

Shifting our lens

This chapter has focused on the role of senior leaders, essentially C-suite and direct reports, in fostering freedom. While leaders have a significant influence over 'the way things are done around here' through their decisions, language, and behaviour, what they pay attention to and reward and how they react to critical incidents, on a day-to-day basis people's experience of work is largely determined by their relationship with their line manager. An executive team can promote all the freedom they like but if a particular manager is selective about how they interpret and implement this locally, then freedom gets filtered out and over time, People Glue is weakened. So, in the final chapter, I'll look at the role of the manager in supporting freedom, some of the tensions that might hamper this, and how you can upskill managers to become effective 'freedom coaches'.

Chapter 14
Freedom coaches

'I would like to be remembered as a person who wanted to be free... so other people would be also free.'

Rosa Parks

Glue spreaders

THE APHORISM THAT people leave their manager not their company generally holds true; even when encountering setbacks at work, people will often stay on if they've got a supportive line manager fighting their corner. Managers play a critical role in nurturing loyalty and commitment because the way they steer the team's work, oversee team members, and influence the immediate working environment directly impacts those individuals' experiences of work. Whether an employee benefits or not from the four freedoms – autonomy, growth, self-expression, and meaningful work – is often determined by how much their manager actively promotes and facilitates these freedoms locally.

Managers today are expected to be adept at responding to a far wider range of situations and expectations than a decade or so ago while still keeping their team on track and managing upwards. This shift in role *hasn't* been matched with a corresponding increase in manager training and upskilling, with damaging consequences. In this chapter, I'll examine what is required of a manager today, how well prepared they are to manage in an environment of greater freedom and why their ability to do so directly influences not just retention, but business performance. I'll set out the forward-looking role of the manager as a 'freedom coach', some points of tension to watch out for, and some guidance on how to support your managers to become successful freedom coaches.

Yesterday and tomorrow

Think back to your first line manager. Unless you're a relatively new entrant into the world of work or were in a peripatetic role, they probably worked near you physically (pandemic aside). Their management responsibilities were likely limited to hiring, assigning tasks, reviewing work outputs, managing performance, grievances and absences, and when necessary, firing or communicating redundancy decisions. They were 'doers' who managed by direct supervision to keep day-to-day operations on track; they weren't expected to provide career coaching, take an interest in your home life or your mental health or, frankly, how fulfilled you felt in your work life. That species of manager has evolved into a very different one today.

Managers are still more likely to be male than female – for every 100 men who received their first promotion to manager in 2024, just 81 women did.[1] These managers are increasingly Millennials managing Gen Zers,* more likely to be working in a hybrid-arrangement and typically staying longer in their role than non-managerial colleagues – the median job tenure for managers is significantly higher at 6.4 years.[2] The amount of freedom a manager has varies by geography: greater freedom and flatter

* Millennials/Gen Y were born between 1981–1996 and Gen Z between 1997–2012.

structures are more prevalent in northern Europe and the US, southern European countries exercise more central control and in Asia more hierarchical structures tend to limit managerial initiative and discretionary decision-making.[3]

Periodically organizations decide it's time to 'strip out' management layers, usually in a bid to cut costs and bureaucracy, and the question of whether we still need managers is hotly debated today. But far from becoming extinct, the new species of manager is proliferating. In the US, management roles are projected to grow by over half a million or 4.7% in the decade to 2029 with a similar trend line in the UK, where a 1.5% increase on today's 8.4 million managers is anticipated.[4]

Managing has become a much more complex job compared to the narrower, more rule-based role of the past. Management by walking around is impossible post-pandemic with the majority of people still wanting and benefiting from hybrid-working. Leaders see managers as key to creating inclusive workplaces while team members expect personalized service and care alongside high-quality management skills, meaning managers have to be adept at talking about health, neurodiversity and disability, microaggressions and psychological safety, mental wellbeing and more. Plus, as AI reshapes the way work is done, the role of the manager is simultaneously being redefined. Advanced analytics tools and the automation of administrative work are freeing up managers to focus on more strategic and human-centric responsibilities: goodbye close supervision, hello cross-functional collaboration and co-ordination. As 'crucial connectors' for team collaboration and effectiveness, managers influence 70% of employee engagement levels.[5] With change as a constant, managers are more involved in implementing transformation efforts and developing team effectiveness, and are expected to demonstrate empathy, facilitation skills and expertise in diagnosing and shaping team culture. Doing this well increases employee motivation, job satisfaction, and feelings of inclusion.

Accidentally unprepared

Given these myriad requirements of a manager today, how well equipped and supported are they to adapt to this new paradigm? The answer is: insufficiently.

One indicator is the low value placed on management skills, as the following indicators and examples in Figure 7 show.

Figure 7 Unprepared managers

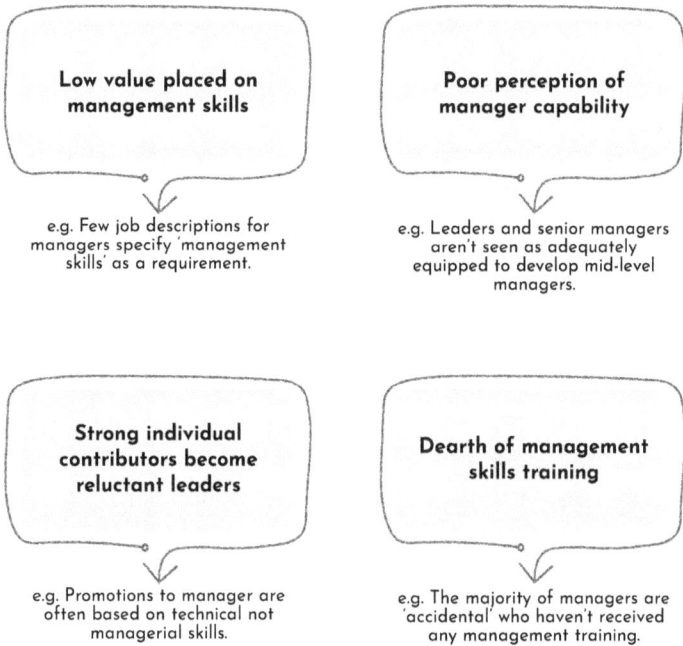

Low value placed on management skills	**Poor perception of manager capability**
e.g. Few job descriptions for managers specify 'management skills' as a requirement.	e.g. Leaders and senior managers aren't seen as adequately equipped to develop mid-level managers.
Strong individual contributors become reluctant leaders	**Dearth of management skills training**
e.g. Promotions to manager are often based on technical not managerial skills.	e.g. The majority of managers are 'accidental' who haven't received any management training.

It should come as no surprise that managers have more negative experiences of work than non-managers and 75% of HR leaders say their managers feel overwhelmed by ever-expanding job descriptions and relentless waves of organizational change.[6] These 'squeezed' managers decry their organization's lack of care for their wellbeing and scant work life balance; they are exhausted by the triple whammy of heavier workloads, tighter budgets, and reduced resources and find it impossible to satisfy both leaders' exhortations and team members' expectations. As you'll see shortly, the consequences of these manager struggles ripple far and wide.

So, we're not preparing current and future managers well enough. On the plus side, however, many managers are more positive about flexible working today, with 75% agreeing that it raises productivity and 62.5% believing that it increases motivation.[7] Not everyone is convinced: some managers embrace it but others say 'I get it, but it's not going to work in my team' and they put it in the 'too difficult' box. It's generally down to luck as to which manager you get.

Linchpins

Managers play a vital role in enabling freedom and strengthening People Glue, so investing in upgrading manager capability will reap extensive rewards for the business as a whole, for individual team members and for managers themselves.

At the macro level, by improving managers' skills they are better able to develop their team members, leading to higher levels of productivity and a better-quality workforce. Multiplied across organizations and industries, this enhances the quality of labour supply which in turn increases economic growth. There is a proven link between management capability and practices and company performance (regardless of sector, size or profitability) whereby improved management capability bolsters market share, productivity and financial performance.[8] So, grow your managers and you grow business success.

If you want an energized, committed workforce then managers are linchpins here too: as well as accounting for 70% of the variance in teams' levels of engagement as we saw above, when managers themselves are positively engaged, employees are more likely to be engaged too.[9] Competent people managers can drive up engagement by setting stretching but motivating goals, holding people accountable for achieving these, providing frequent, constructive feedback, actively coaching their team members on the day-to-day delivery, coaxing out higher levels of creativity and innovation, recognizing, and rewarding contributions in a timely way, and supporting their longer-term development.

Managers also play an outsize role in fostering a positive work culture. While the broader organizational culture, the ability to work flexibly and targeted diversity and inclusion initiatives all contribute to people feeling supported and included at work, the single most influential factor is... having a supportive manager.[10] A manager's effectiveness influences the quality of people's relationships at work, their productivity, and their level of job satisfaction.[11]

Finally, there is clear evidence that managers directly impact levels of retention and turnover. Having an ineffective or unsupportive boss causes people to leave; in a survey of over 3,000 UK workers, 67% had left or were considering exiting because of a bad manager,[12] while half of us who say our bosses can't manage well are planning to quit within the next 12 months.[13] Frustratingly for employers, a good proportion of leavers believe that proactive action from their manager could have averted their exit. While incompetent or ill-prepared managers weaken People Glue, capable managers actively strengthen it. Repeated positive interactions with managers can reduce preventable exits by around a third and quadruple the likelihood of those employees feeling engaged while positive recognition by the manager substantially reduces the individual's chances of resigning after two years.[14]

The manager as freedom coach

We've seen above how managers are critical to team and business performance yet are likely to be under-skilled for their managerial role. So, how can a manager lead and support their team effectively so that it thrives in a high-freedom environment? Within the organization-wide framework of parameters, programmes, and practices set out in the previous chapter, what should the manager's role focus on and what capabilities do they need to be successful?

If you're serious about creating People Glue in your organization, you need to equip your managers to become *freedom coaches*. Not supervisors, not managers-by-walking-around, not just technically strong colleagues but able to empower the team and get the best out of people, individually and collectively. To become freedom coaches, managers need to create *clarity*, act with *care*, and demonstrate *constancy*. Let's explore each capability in turn and discover what that means in practice.

Creating clarity

Enabling freedom doesn't mean handing over complete autonomy to do whatever people want or to act as they please – the whole team needs to know what work is to be done, how, by whom and when, and equally importantly, what is *not* within their remit or acceptable ways of working. A useful practical model here is the BART framework consisting of boundary, authority, role and task:

- Establishing *boundaries* means clarifying timescales, the scope of tasks and the limits of the team's work, escalating bigger issues or bottlenecks where necessary, being aware of what else is going on in the organization and securing cross-boundary input.
- Ensuring *authority* is about allocating work clearly to team members and encouraging them to exercise their full authority in leading or executing this (without exceeding this authority).
- Clarifying *roles*, both formally designated responsibilities and informally assumed or agreed ones such as being the team social organizer, the constructive critic or the peacemaker.

- Defining *tasks* includes commissioning work, specifying expected speed, quality and degree of original thinking required, plus awareness of the way in which people are working together on tasks.

Acting with care

To offer greater freedom and build a 'sticky' team culture, managers have to understand and work to meet individual team members' needs, as far as possible. This requires managers first to work on their own self-awareness and emotional intelligence and second, learn how to deploy these psychological 'tools' to get the best out of the team. They can demonstrate respect and care for team members' opinions, ideas, concerns, ambitions, growth, and wellbeing by:

- Paying attention to team dynamics and how the team is functioning.
- Checking and surfacing assumptions.
- Approaching difficult conversations thoughtfully and with integrity.
- Asking open questions like 'what's your take on this?', 'what's important to you here?', 'how can I best help you?', and 'what do you need right now?'.
- Listening carefully to the answers.
- Admitting honestly when they don't have all the answers and committing to actions they *can* take that might help.
- Calling out exclusionary behaviours.

By acting with care in these ways managers can better harness the team's diversity of thought, experience, and personality; encourage colleagues to step outside their comfort zones or step up; help people navigate the emotional rollercoaster of organizational uncertainty and change; and support individuals through career setbacks or major life events.

Demonstrating constancy

While consistency in a manager's actions and decisions strengthens stability and fairness, if they want to foster freedom and grow glue managers need to demonstrate *constancy* over the longer-term, both on a 1:1 basis and with the team as a whole. How do they do this? By regularly checking in with people, by keeping a constructive dialogue going about 'how we/you are doing, what's going well, what's not and why'; by coaching people in their development; by monitoring and acknowledging effort, progress and achievement; and by reinforcing positive ways of working through meaningful recognition and rewards.

With individual team members, managers can:

- Honour commitments they've made.
- Encourage agency, e.g., 'take ownership of your career path, growth and potential, we're here to support you'.
- Offer regular feedback in real-time, fuelling people's confidence that they are adding value and helping them adapt their approach when needed.
- Agree a cadence of check-ins that suits each individual, e.g., frequent and light-touch; less frequent and more in-depth; or varying according to work intensity.

With the whole team, managers can:

- Facilitate informal team agreements to establish consensus about how they'll work together.*
- Establish a rhythm of operational touchpoints e.g., team meetings, progress trackers, post-deliverable learning, social time together, and celebrating beginnings, endings and successes.

* For an example, visit my website www.helenbeedham.com.

- Have regular 'standback' sessions to review how well they are working and what they want to change.[†]
- Lead horizon-scanning sessions to spot trends or developments early and build preparedness and resilience.

By demonstrating constancy, managers can reliably follow up on concerns or frustrations, nip potential risks or issues in the bud and develop the group into a high-performing team.

Supporting the shift

The first step in helping your managers to make the shift towards becoming a freedom coach is to define what it means to be a manager in your organization *today and in the future*, and how this is different to before. Engage your current managers in working up this new definition, so they feel involved in the process instead of feeling like this is being done 'to them', they begin to accept why change is needed and can explore what it means for them.

Second, invest in upgrading your current manager development offering. A comprehensive offering should include training sessions, learning opportunities, and group coaching programmes on the following:

- Meeting and workshop facilitation skills.
- Understanding group dynamics.
- Using personality profiling tools.
- Handling difficult or sensitive conversations, including giving feedback.
- Useful models for team development and effectiveness.
- Managing boundaries for self and team.
- Basic coaching techniques.
- Listening and empathy skills.
- Basic change management skills.

[†] Ask me about my 'time-intelligent team' workshops.

- 'Time intelligence' skills for self and team to help them cope with time pressure, balance competing demands, increase their productivity and enjoyment.[‡]

One property consultancy has developed a programme to grow awareness of what a good manager looks like. They invite roughly 100 colleagues identified as potential stars of the future to participate, running the programme every two years. This is a conscious, focused way of investing in a diverse, high-performing group drawn from across the business and growing them into highly capable managers.

Alongside your formal programmes you can:

- Initiate action learning groups bringing managers together periodically for some self-reflection, to share how they are practising the new skills, and to inspire reluctant managers to give it a try. This peer-based approach builds confidence to manage differently.
- Provide temporary, hands-on support to each team, or selected teams. One client of mine invited me in to run sessions with all of their teams and hold 1:1 coaching calls with the managers pre- and post-workshops. This enabled the managers to learn from 'live' team development and facilitation and grew their confidence in leading similar conversations themselves.
- Introduce a formal manager mentoring scheme, pairing up capable, experienced managers with first-time managers.

Third, bring your new manager definition into all your people processes:

- Specify the required management skills as an essential criteria when you're hiring managers from outside and within.

[‡] Find out more at www.helenbeedham.com.

- Link the skills to promotion criteria, progression, and access to attractive opportunities – make these skills seen as desirable and a 'must have' to advance towards senior leadership.
- Professionalize management skills through internal or external accreditation, which will be valued by both aspiring and experienced managers.

Fourth, get a handle on how your managers are performing versus your new benchmark. Ways to do this include:

- Inviting team members to rate their manager via 180° feedback.
- Identifying who is delivering on both the target outputs *and* building a functioning team.
- Including the 'how' of management (how they create clarity, act with care, and demonstrate constancy) in their personal performance objectives and reviews.
- Gathering insights from your attrition data, exit interviews and any leavers research.
- Mapping your managers on a quadrant, using all your manager performance data, to identify who's making the shift and who needs greater support.

Finally, watch out for some tensions that may need addressing. In growing your People Glue, there's just as big a risk that managers, like anyone else, feel left to sink or swim in an environment of greater freedom. They might overcompensate by trying to do all the work in order to prove themselves. They may overexpress concern for team members' wellbeing by reducing their autonomy, as an anxious parent might with their teenager. Talented managers comfortable with freedom are often good at creating (potentially disempowering) structure for teams so the challenge is for these managers to manage autonomously too. Finally, be mindful that by growing awareness of what a good manager or freedom coach is, you're opening people's eyes to practices around them that may fall short. So, if you do introduce a programme to grow great managers, have in your mind right from the start the question of how you can quickly and easily scale this up.

Advice for leaders

The following recommendations may help you embark on your shift to upskill managers into freedom coaches:

1. Calculate your potential business gains from enhancing manager capability; you can use the World Management Survey outcomes[15] as a basis for this.
2. Invite your Head of HR or Talent or a trusted external consultant to identify the gaps in your manager development offering, the priorities to close, and ballpark budget required.
3. Talk to your CIO (Chief Information Officer) or CTO (Chief Technology Officer) about how the adoption of new technology can help raise manager capability and reduce the low value-adding elements of their role today.
4. Set an example of empowerment with managers who report into you. Focus on the big picture and the front line, don't micromanage the middle. Ask your manager for feedback on how well you're balancing structure versus freedom for them.
5. Have honest conversations with your managers about niceness, specifically how a desire to be nice can make managers less effective, less trusted and less respected, so getting out of your comfort zones here is essential.

Advice for individuals

If you're a manager:

1. Reflect on the role of a freedom coach described above and the feedback you've received over the past one to two years. Where do you see your strengths and weaknesses?

2. Review the manager development offering in 'Supporting the shift' above; which of these have you already benefited from? Which would be the priorities, from your perspective and your employer's, in terms of what you might access next?

3. Invite a handful of other managers to have an informal chat about how they find the role of a manager and how they've noticed this evolving.

4. Look into getting external accreditation for your manager skills if your employer doesn't offer this.

If you're not a manager:

1. Think about how you're promoting trust and empowerment within your team. For example, frequently copying your manager on emails to colleagues can halve the level of trust colleagues feel towards you, so only email colleagues that are directly involved and update your manager separately.

2. If your manager frustrates you or fails to support you sufficiently, use your agency rather than falling back on self-pity or recriminations. Practice active listening, set clear expectations, provide constructive feedback, show you're aligned to the manager's objectives, and demonstrate your commitment to the team's goals. These are all ways to positively influence your manager.

3. When your manager fails to create clarity, act with care or demonstrate constancy, stop to look at the full picture before judging them negatively. What has their week been like? What stressors might they be dealing with? Is this a one-off incident or the latest of many examples of managerial inadequacy?

4. If you aspire to be a manager look at how the role of a manager is defined in your organization and what training and development is provided to new managers. Ask your

manager how they found the transition into their first managerial role and what helped.

No rolling back

In Part 4, we've looked at a practical framework for operationalizing freedom in your organization; how to respond when freedom falters; the ways in which leaders can explore their personal relationship with freedom and grow People Glue through their choice of words and actions; and how organizations can better equip people managers to manage freedom, with potentially transformative results for your workforce and your business. Let me leave you now with a few closing thoughts.

Conclusion

'None but the brave deserve the fair.'

John Dryden

Getting to here

IN THE PRECEDING chapters, I have defined what I mean by
People Glue and evidenced the direct link between freedom,
retention, and improved business performance. You've discovered how to assess the state of your People Glue today
and how well your organization currently stacks up against
the four freedoms that people value most. I've described the
parameters, programmes, and practices that enable you to offer
greater freedom to your employees in a way that fires up deep
commitment and discretionary effort. And I've argued in favour
of curbing the understandable urge to cling tightly to personal
and systemic controls and instead, through your own example
and by upskilling managers into freedom coaches, to let go, secure
in the knowledge that with the right structure, accountability,
support and connection people will cohere around your purpose,
concentrate their energies on achieving your shared goals and
commit to the ways of working that you value.

Good intentions, greater insights

'No-one knowingly does evil' claimed Socrates in his legal self-defense when on trial in 399BC for corruption and impiety. With this statement he was advocating that people generally commit evil out of ignorance rather than hatred or selfishness and that with the continuous pursuit of better knowledge of ourselves and others, we can lead a more virtuous life.

I don't believe that organizations restrict freedom out of a deliberate desire to exercise unilateral control or make people's working lives harder or less enjoyable. I *do* believe the majority of leaders are intensely focused on creating the optimum conditions for their employees to thrive and perform at their best; they're just constantly under pressure to meet exacting expectations in often difficult or disruptive circumstances while balancing many competing priorities. From what's worked before and elsewhere, from their own reflective or coaching practice and from business books like this, leaders are continuously seeking better knowledge about how to create a winning, human-centric organization, putting this into practice, and along the way, inspiring others.

Three hopes

If you're a leader reading this and thinking about your business and employees, I hope that:

1. *People Glue* has encouraged you to be bolder in offering your employees more freedom; to try things that as a leadership team you've shied away from before; and to feel more confident in managing the risks that might rear their heads along the way.
2. You feel better prepared to respond appropriately to unexpected consequences and bumps in the road as you advance and if it feels like two steps forward, one step back, keep the faith. This is a long-term game so be patient, keep investing in this with your time, effort, people,

and financial resources and don't expect an immediate return on that investment; year on year, the benefits will materialize and multiply, generating further opportunities to keep enhancing your freedom framework and seeing that translate into a happier, more productive workforce and improved retention.

3. *People Glue* helps position you and your organization to be on the front foot to respond successfully to present opportunities and challenges and future developments, with a highly capable and committed workforce powering your progress.

If you're an individual thinking about your own work and career, then I hope that:

1. You've gained greater clarity about what's most important to you, now and in the future. If you're benefiting from those things today, that's wonderful – celebrate this and make the most of it. If you've been lacking these things, feeling stuck or dissatisfied, then I hope you're clearer about what you want to change.

2. You're thinking bigger in terms of your own work and career options and feeling more confident about opening up or exploring new possibilities in your current organization, on the side of your day job or elsewhere.

3. You feel better equipped to approach conversations with colleagues, friends, loved ones – even your boss – about their own work lives, to help them navigate their own roles and career choices positively. All of us can promote and support freedom at work every day in our own spheres of influence.

The future at our fingertips

Freedom at work matters to people and to businesses today as much – if not more – than it ever has done. I believe we're in a fortunate position, generationally speaking, in that we've got more options work-wise than perhaps our parents and certainly our grandparents enjoyed, when geographic proximity to jobs mattered enormously, work norms were rigid and prescriptive, and global jobs boards and networking opportunities simply didn't exist. Provided we're prepared to invest the effort, we can pursue the roles, locations, and working patterns that provide us with the work life and lifestyle that we value or aspire to. Access to a dazzling, infinite set of possibilities is right here in our hands.

There are exciting futures ahead too for businesses hungry to grow, despite the challenges and uncertainties I described in the Introduction. With disruption and new technology come unforeseen opportunities, with a global market comes competitors to keep you sharp and new customers to serve. If you can attract and retain the people and skills you need to succeed, these prizes are there for the taking.

But I also firmly believe that organizations who are tightening up on freedoms today will see a steady outflow of talent impacting their ability to innovate, compete, and be nimble tomorrow, while eating into their profit margins. Their market advantages will be whittled away as they see competitors offering greater freedom attract the brightest workers and reap the rewards.

So, building a 'sticky' organization is about the hard facts of business success or failure – *and* it's about more than that. While we can rationally debate the pros and cons of greater freedom of work, this is fundamentally about human lives and emotions, the potential for individual and collective self-actualization, and the creation of healthy, vibrant communities.

By giving your employees greater freedom, you can become the most attractive company in your field. Achieve big, hairy, audacious goals together. Make a healthy, sustainable profit. You can break boundaries and forge new frontiers of knowledge and expertise. Achieve breakthroughs in science and medicine, contribute to a flourishing economy. Protect our natural world; lift people out of poverty and take care of the vulnerable. Leave a lasting legacy.

That's the power of People Glue.

Acknowledgements

I T'S HERE THAT I lift the lid a little on how *People Glue* came into being and I can publicly thank all those who have contributed to this outcome. If you have an image in your head of me sitting in glorious isolation with a towel over my head, bashing out chapters, it's partly accurate. That's one half of the writing story, where I was distilling down, organizing, and articulating the mass of ideas and insights that I wanted to share with you.

The other half of the story is very different; it involved many conversations with a wonderful variety of people who generously shared their time and wisdom with me. Their perspectives and stories were fascinating and helped me enormously in shaping *People Glue*'s message and contents.

I am especially grateful to the following leaders who spoke with me before and during the months of writing:

Mark Arian, formerly Chief Executive Officer, Korn Ferry Consulting.

Steven Baert, Chief People Officer, GE Vernova.

Keith Barker, Managing Director UK & Ireland, Weinerberger.

Akanksha Bindal, General Manager International Business, Pernod Ricard India.

Chris Brook, Group Chief Operating Officer, BMS Group.

Claire Campbell, Chief Executive Officer, Timewise.

Stephen Clifton, UK Managing Partner, Knight Frank.

Winnie Doeswijk, Global Head of Organization Development, Siemens.

Julie Doleman, FTSE100 Managing Director & P&L Leader.

Ruth Handcock OBE, Chief Executive Officer, Octopus Money.

Jaya Louvre, Global Head of Talent Acquisition & Diversity, Withers LLP.

Dr Ajit Menon, Strategic Advisor and former Chief People Officer.

Eleanor Minshall, HR Director UK & Ireland, Weinerberger.

Susi Pitura, International COO and Country Head, UK, Cohen & Steers.

Tim Roberts, Chief Executive Officer, Henry Boot PLC.

Tom Shaw, Head of Organization Effectiveness, The Economist.

Dominique Sherry, Chief of Staff, Low Carbon.

Jennifer Sundberg, Founder and Advisory Board Member, Board Intelligence.

Brent Taylor, Chief Executive Officer, Barrows.

Raj Tulsiani, Chief Executive Officer, Green Park.

Kelly Whitfield, Partner, Teacher Stern.

Simon Wilson, CEO, Markel Insurance.

Additionally, I'd like to acknowledge Anna Campagna, Jennifer Halliday, Dr Julie Humphreys, Michelle Newton, Hannah Rowland, Sharon Spice, Leo Stoll, and Alison Trauttmansdorff in brokering introductions – thank you for opening doors and recommending me so generously.

Back in July 2024, it was with some trepidation that I put forward my idea for *People Glue* to my publisher Alison Jones. It had been brewing in my head for several months and after a writing retreat to put some initial structure around it, I sent her a one paragraph overview of the concept. I was blown away by her immediate 'yes!' – thank you Alison for seeing the potential in that scrappy first articulation and for believing I could turn this into a fully-fledged book that I hope will spark constructive conversations and positive change in the world of work. My thanks also to editor Susannah Fountain for her discerning and invaluable suggestions, project manager Kelly Winter at Newgen Publishing UK, Shell Cooper and Michelle Charman at Practical Inspiration Publishing for checking in regularly and your patience in answering my various questions, and Rex Elston and Sarah Hodgen for marketing support.

The second scariest step – after getting a 'yes' from Alison and cementing the deadline for writing 50,000 words – was sharing the draft manuscript with its very first audience. Thank you to my beta readers John Beedham, Dr Julie Humphreys, Eleanor Minshall, and Margaret Ruiseal for taking the time to absorb it, share your comments, and suggest how I could improve it. I am immensely grateful and hope you recognize your feedback reflected in this final version.

Coming up with the cover design for *People Glue* was trickier than I anticipated, and I appreciated all the honest opinions on early versions from friends, family, and my LinkedIn network. Huge thanks to Ella Coleman at Mozarella for her original artwork and skilful cover design which beautifully conveys my message of soaring possibility, and for the illustrations inside. On the research side, Eliana Strauss was a delight to work with and instrumental in conducting the primary and secondary research on which I drew heavily while writing *People Glue*; thank you to all who responded to and shared my 'Freedom at work' survey in late 2024. Early into the writing process, I realized that offering freedom to adults in the world of work shares numerous parallels with offering freedom to adolescent offspring, and so I gratefully tapped into parenting expert Anita Cleare's skills and sagacity to unpack this analogy further. Alice Sheldon, thank you for our weekly check-ins which always cheered my Mondays and played a vital role in keeping me on track right to the end.

To all my family and friends at home and at work who have asked me 'how's it going?', your interest and encouragement helped me to keep motoring on and I hope I didn't bore you with long detailed answers when you were praying for a short one. And no, I haven't started book three yet.

Last and closest to my heart, thank you to my mother Judith for your constant love and support and to my beloved Beedham peeps – John, William, Rebecca, and Isabella. You are wonderful beyond words.

Notes

Introduction

[1] Cautious to Confident: PwC Pulse Survey, 18 October 2022. www.pwc.com/us/growththroughrecession.

[2] Research conducted by Remote across 544 employers in December 2022. https://remote.com/blog/employee-turnover#employee-turnover-rates-have-increased-by-8-7-since-2019.

Chapter 1: People Glue

[1] What do people really want in their work? Meaning and stability. *American Psychological Association*, 4 March 2024. www.apa.org/monitor/2024/01/trends-meaning-stability-workplaces.

[2] Putting Purpose to Work: A study of purpose in the workplace, PwC. www.pwc.com/us/en/about-us/corporate-responsibility/assets/pwc-putting-purpose-to-work-purpose-survey-report.pdf.

[3] Transform into a radically human organization, Korn Ferry Consulting. www.kornferry.com/insights/featured-topics/organizational-transformation/transform-into-radically-human-organization.

[4] State of the Global Workplace 2023 Report, Gallup. www.gallup.com/workplace/349484/state-of-the-global-workplace-2022-report.aspx.

Chapter 2: Why people stay

[1] Employee tenure in 2024, US Bureau of Labor Statistics. www.bls. gov/news.release/pdf/.

[2] Employee Retention & Attraction Indicators, Gallup. 2024. www. gallup.com/467702/indicator-employee-retention-attraction.aspx.

[3] *How to reduce employee turnover with a strong talent retention strategy*, Remote. com, https://remote.com/blog/employee-turnover#employee-turnover-rates-have-increased-by-8-7-since-2019.

[4] LinkedIn Learning Report, 2023. https://learning.linkedin.com/ resources/workplace-learning-report-2023.

[5] Global Insights Workforce 2024 report, Korn Ferry. www.kornferry. com/insights/featured-topics/workforce-management/workforce-planning-insights.

[6] Gallup's Employee Attraction & Retention Indicators. www.gallup.com/467702/indicator-employee-retention-attraction.aspx; their State of the Global Workplace 2024 Report and LinkedIn and Microsoft's research AI at Work Is Here. Now Comes the Hard Part, 2024. www.microsoft.com/en-us/worklab/work-trend-index/ai-at-work-is-here-now-comes-the-hard-part.

[7] Ten Top Reasons for Employee Turnover & How To Prevent It, AiHR. www.aihr.com/blog/what-drives-employee-turnover/.

[8] Toxic Culture is Driving the Great Resignation, MIT Sloan Management Review, 11 January 2022. https://sloanreview.mit.edu/article/toxic-culture-is-driving-the-great-resignation/.

[9] Who Is Leaving and Why? The Dynamics of High-Quality Human Capital Outflows, *Academy of Management*, 19 December 2023. https:// journals.aom.org/doi/10.5465/amj.2021.1327.

[10] Why Women Leave: How gender influences retention, a study comprising over 4,000 women and 1,400 men. Encompass Equality, May 2024. www.encompassequality.com/.

[11] Global Insights Workforce 2024 report, Korn Ferry. www.kornferry.com/insights/featured-topics/workforce-management/workforce-planning-insights.

[12] 42% of Employee Turnover Is Preventable but Often Ignored, Gallup, 10 July 2024. www.gallup.com/workplace/646538/employee-turnover-preventable-often-ignored.aspx.

Chapter 3: Why retention matters

[1] Organizational Wellbeing Report 2023, Gallagher. www.ajg.com/us/2023-us-workforce-trends-report-series-organizational-wellbeing/.

[2] Attraction and Retention in a Post COVID-19 Era, IBIS. www.ibiweb.org/resources/attraction-and-retention-in-a-post-covid-19-era.

[3] Building the Agile Future: 2023 Workplace Learning Report, LinkedIn, 2023. https://learning.linkedin.com/content/dam/me/learning/en-us/pdfs/workplace-learning-report/LinkedIn-Learning_Workplace-Learning-Report-2023-EN.pdf.

[4] Live a Little: Baby-boomers are loaded. Why are they so stingy? *The Economist*, 1 June 2024. www.economist.com/finance-and-economics/2024/05/26/baby-boomers-are-loaded-why-are-they-so-stingy.

[5] UK Business Chiefs: GenAI a positive disruptor and increased expectation on full return to in office working. KPMG, September 2024. https://kpmg.com/uk/en/home/media/press-releases/2024/09/uk-business-chiefs.html.

[6] Top 5 Priorities for HR Leaders in 2025, Gartner, 2024. www.gartner.com/en/human-resources/trends/top-priorities-for-hr-leaders.

[7] Satisfied Workers Stay: The Benefits of Employee Satisfaction on Retention in Europe. Glassdoor, 8 November 2022. www.glassdoor.com/research/european-satisfied-workers-stay/.

[8] It pays to stay. HR Review, 12 April 2018. https://hrreview.co.uk/hr-news/recruitment/it-pays-to-stay-workers-who-spend-2-to-3-years-in-first-job-earn-higher-salaries-over-career/110810.

[9] 'Quiet hiring: why managers are recruiting from their own ranks', *The Financial Times*, 10 February 2024. www.ft.com/content/6c8ddab2-ca1d-4817-b705-eae6608a07b2.

[10] Employee Attraction & Retention Indicators, Gallup, 2024. www.gallup.com/467702/indicator-employee-retention-attraction.aspx.

[11] 15 employee retention statistics and figures to know ahead of 2025 (UK), Stribe, November 2024. https://stribehq.com/resources/employee-retention-statistics-uk/.

[12] How Diversity Can Drive Innovation, *Harvard Business Review*, December 2013. https://hbr.org/2013/12/how-diversity-can-drive-innovation.

[13] Workforce of the future: the competing forces shaping 2030, PwC, 2017. www.pwc.com/gx/en/services/workforce/publications/workforce-of-the-future.html.

[14] Workplace Learning Report 2024, LinkedIn, 2024. https://learning.linkedin.com/resources/workplace-learning-report.

Chapter 5: The freedom evolution

[1] The Business of Being Brilliant podcast, series 6, episode 7 on 'Understanding our social brain' with Professor Robin Dunbar, 23 October 2023. www.helenbeedham.com/podcast/s6-robin-dunbar.

[2] Eight in ten workers think AI will impact their jobs, and not necessarily for the better, *Unleash*, 10 July 2024. www.unleash.ai/automation/adp-8-in-10-workers-think-ai-will-impact-their-jobs-and-not-necessarily-for-the-better/.

[3] The constant mirror: Self-view and attitudes to virtual meetings, *Science Direct*, 3 December 2021. www.sciencedirect.com/science/article/abs/pii/S0747563221004337.

[4] *Global Talent Retention: Understanding employee turnover around the world*, by David G. Allen and James M. Vardaman. Emerald Publishing Ltd, March 2024. www.emerald.com/insight/publication/doi/10.1108/9781839092930.

[5] 'We aren't your reincarnation!' workplace motivation across X, Y and Z generations, by Ali B. Mahmoud, Leonora Fuxman, Iris Mohr, William D. Reisel, Nicholas Grigoriou. *International Journal of Manpower*, 17 June 2020. www.emerald.com/insight/content/doi/10.1108/ijm-09-2019-0448/full/html.

[6] Generative AI could raise global GDP by 7%, Goldman Sachs, 5 April 2023. www.goldmansachs.com/insights/articles/generative-ai-could-raise- global-gdp-by-7-percent.html.

Chapter 6: Anti-freedom forces

[1] Navigating the new geopolitical uncertainty, McKinsey & Co, 16 January 2025. www.mckinsey.com/capabilities/geopolitics/our-insights/navigating-the-new-geopolitical-uncertainty.

[2] Working still harder, by By Francis Green, Alan Felstead, Duncan Gailie. *ILR Review*, 27 January 2021. https://journals.sagepub.com/doi/10.1177/0019793920977850?icid=int.sj-abstract.citing-articles.1&.

[3] Do You Know How Your Teams Get Work Done? by Rohan Narayana Murty, Rajath B. Das, Scott Duke Kominers, Arjun Narayan, Suraj Srinivasan, Tarun Khanna and Kartik Hosanagar. *Harvard Business Review*, 1 December 2021. https://hbr.org/2021/12/do-you-know-how-your-teams-get-work-done?.

Chapter 7: Autonomy

[1] Work-life balance tops pay: Randstad's WorkMonitor reveals new workplace baseline, Randstad, January 2025. In this annual survey of 26,000 workers in 35 markets across Europe, Asia Pacific and the Americas, for the first time in 22 years' work-life balance (83%) surpassed pay (82%) as the leading motivator. www.randstad.com/press/2025/work-life-balance-tops-pay-randstads-workmonitor-reveals/.

[2] Randstad WorkMonitor 2023: flexible, but stable, Randstad, 2023. https://workforceinsights.randstad.com/workmonitor-2023.

[3] The state of flexible work, Scoop Q4 2024, www.flexindex.com/stats.

[4] Workforce 2024, Korn Ferry. www.kornferry.com/insights/featured-topics/workforce-management/workforce-planning-insights.

[5] Hybrid working from home improves retention without damaging performance, by Nicholas Bloom, Ruobin Han, James Liang. Nature.com, 12 June 2024. www.nature.com/articles/s41586-024-07500-2.

[6] Future Forum Pulse February 2023, Future Forum. https://futureforum.com/research/future-forum-pulse-winter-2022-2023-snapshot/#how-does-burnout-affect-retention.

[7] The Surprising Impact of Meeting-Free Days, *MIT Sloan Management Review*, 18 January 2022. https://sloanreview.mit.edu/article/the-surprising-impact-of-meeting-free-days/.

[8] Hybrid working from home improves retention without damaging performance, *Nature*, 12 June 2024. www.nature.com/articles/s41586-024-07500-2.

[9] Return to Office Mandates research analysing 127 Standard & Poor 500 companies, *SSRN*, 25 December 2023. https://papers.ssrn.com/sol3/papers.cfm?abstract_id=4675401.

[10] Office Mandates Could Drive More Bosses Than Workers to Quit, *Forbes*, 15 May 2024, refers to a Gartner survey of 3,500 employees. www.forbes.com/sites/jenamcgregor/2024/05/15/office-mandates-could-drive-more-bosses-than-workers-to-quit/?sh=2c1af78f9e00.

Chapter 8: Growth

[1] Future of Work: The global talent crunch, Korn Ferry. www.kornferry.com/insights/this-week-in-leadership/talent-crunch-future-of-work.

[2] Employer investment in upskilling and reskilling in a changing economy, the Learning & Work Institute. https://learningandwork.org.uk/resources/research-and-reports/employer-investment-in-upskilling-and-reskilling-in-a-changing-economy/.

[3] The everyone economy: CMI's plan for sharing work, opportunity and success, 1 July 2022. www.managers.org.uk/knowledge-and-insights/research/everyone-economy/.

[4] Building the agile future: 2023 Workplace Learning Report, LinkedIn. https://learning.linkedin.com/content/dam/me/learning/en-us/pdfs/workplace-learning-report/LinkedIn-Learning_Workplace-Learning-Report-2023-EN.pdf.

[5] Three ways work experience outsmarts formal education for professional development, *World Economic Forum*. www.weforum.org/agenda/2022/06/3-ways-in-which-work-experience-enhances-the-value-of-human-capital.

[6] Enjoying Work Matters More Than You May Realize, *BCG*, 13 February 2024. www.bcg.com/publications/2024/joy-at-work-matters-more-than-you-realize.

Chapter 9: Self-expression

[1] Unconfuse me with Bill Gates podcast, episode 7 with Hannah Ritchie, 1 February 2024. www.gatesnotes.com/Unconfuse-Me-podcast-with-guest-Hannah-Ritchie.

[2] State of the global workforce 2024, Gallup, October 2022. www.gallup.com/workplace/349484/state-of-the-global-workplace.aspx.

[3] 'Great Attrition' or 'Great Attraction'? The choice is yours, McKinsey, 8 September 2021. www.mckinsey.com/capabilities/people-and-organizational-performance/our-insights/great-attrition-or-great-attraction-the-choice-is-yours.

[4] The everyone economy: CMI's plan for sharing work, opportunity and success, Chartered Management Institute, 1 July 2022. www.managers.org.uk/knowledge-and-insights/research/everyone-economy/.

[5] Global Insights Workforce 2024 report, Korn Ferry. www.kornferry.com/insights/featured-topics/workforce-management/workforce-planning-insights.

[6] Toxic Culture is driving the Great Resignation, *MIT Sloan Management Review*, 11 January 2022. https://sloanreview.mit.edu/article/toxic-culture-is-driving-the-great-resignation/.

7 Exploring the Positive Impact of Secure Base Leadership, *Human Capital Leadership Review*, 30 September 2024. www.innovativehuman capital.com/article/exploring-the-positive-impact-of-secure-base-leadership-work-engagement-as-a-mediator-in-fostering.

8 Team Health Monitor. www.atlassian.com/team-playbook/health-monitor.

Chapter 10: Meaningful work

1 What do people really want in their work? Meaning and stability. A survey of 2,515 employed adults conducted on behalf of the American Psychological Association, 4 March 2024. www.apa.org/monitor/2024/01/trends-meaning-stability-workplaces.

2 What is meaningful work? Kings Business School, Kings College London, April 2023. www.kcl.ac.uk/business/assets/pdf/what-is-mea ningful-work-and-does-it-matter.pdf.

3 What makes work meaningful? WISERD (Wales Institute of Social and Economic Research and Data), April 2025. https://wiserd.ac.uk/publication/what-makes-work-meaningful/.

4 Hybrid Work Is Just Work. Are We Doing It Wrong? Microsoft's 2022 Work Trend Index surveying over 20,000 employees in 11 countries, 20 September 2022. www.microsoft.com/en-us/worklab/work-trend-index/hybrid-work-is-just-work.

5 Bayer CEO: Corporate bureaucracy belongs in the 19th century. Here's how we're fighting it, Fortune.com, 21 March 2024. https://fortune.com/2024/03/21/bayer-ceo-bill-anderson-corporate-bureaucr acy-19th-century-leadership/.

6 Chatty colleagues are biggest productivity killer. *People Management*, 5 February 2024. www.peoplemanagement.co.uk/article/1860267/chatty-colleagues-biggest-productivity-killer-survey-finds-%E2%80%93-hr-achieve-balance.

7 How Will Artificial Intelligence Affect Jobs 2024–2030, *Nextford*, 10 January 2024. www.nexford.edu/insights/how-will-ai-affect-jobs.

8 Women @ Work 2024: A Global Outlook; research involving 5,000 women across 10 countries, Deloitte, April 2024. www.deloitte.com/content/dam/assets-shared/docs/collections/2024/deloitte-women-at-work-2024-a-global-outlook.pdf?dl=2.

9 The state of work 2023, Slack. https://d34u8crftukxnk.cloudfront. net/slackpress/prod/sites/6/State-Work-Report.en-US.pdf.

10 The mindlessness of organizational behaviour, *Sage Journals*, 1988.

11 Breaking Boredom: Interrupting the residual effect of state boredom on future productivity, *Journal of Applied Psychology*, 2024. https://psycnet. apa.org/record/2024-46936-001.

12 Prioritizing the health of female employees is a strategic imperative, McKinsey & World Economic Forum, March 2024. www.weforum. org/agenda/2024/03/womens-mental-health-is-a-strategic-imperative-heres-how-employers-can-bolster-it-today/?emailType=Agenda% 20Weekly, and Mental health and employers, Deloitte research, May 2024. www.deloitte.com/uk/en/services/consulting/research/mental-health-and-employers-the-case-for-employers-to-invest-in-supporting-working-parents-and-a-mentally-health-workplace.html.

Chapter 11: Freedom framework

1 3M's website: www.3m.co.uk/3M/en_GB/careers/culture/15-percent-culture/.

2 Mindset: changing the way you think to fulfil your potential, Carol Dweck, Robinson 2012. https://uk.bookshop.org/p/books/mindset-updated-edition-changing-the-way-you-think-to-fulfil-your-potential-dr-carol-dweck/3479142?ean=9781472139955.

3 The Business of Being Brilliant podcast, series 6, episode 7 on 'Understanding our social brain' with Professor Robin Dunbar, 23 October 2023. www.helenbeedham.com/podcast/s6-robin-dunbar.

4 Dunning-Kruger effect, www.britannica.com/science/Dunning-Kruger-effect.

5 The Global State of Social Connections, Meta & Gallup, 2023. www. gallup.com/analytics/509675/state-of-social-connections.aspx.

Chapter 12: When freedom falters

1 3M's website: www.3m.co.uk/3M/en_GB/careers/culture/15-percent-culture/.

2 Return to Office Mandates and Brain Drain, *SSRN*, 23 November 2024. https://papers.ssrn.com/sol3/papers.cfm?abstract_id=5031481.

Chapter 13: Leading freedom

[1] 2025 Edelman Trust Barometer: Trust and the crisis of grievance. www.edelman.com/trust/2025/trust-barometer.

[2] *Living your Dying*, Stanley Keleman, Random House, 1976.

[3] The Ladder of Inference: Building self-awareness to be a better human-centered leader, Craig Dickerson. *Harvard Business Review*, May 2024. www.harvardbusiness.org/the-ladder-of-inference-building-self-awareness-to-be-a-better-human-centered-leader/#_edn1.

[4] *Resistance to Change – Why it Matters and What to Do About It*, Rick Maurer. https://rickmaurer.com/articles/resistance-to-change-why-it-matters/.

[5] Alice Sheldon offers a free downloadable list of needs on her website: www.needs-understanding.com.

Chapter 14: Freedom coaches

[1] Women in the Workplace 2024: The 10th anniversary report, McKinsey & Co and Lean In, 2024. www.mckinsey.com/featured-insights/diversity-and-inclusion/women-in-the-workplace.

[2] Why everyone's focusing on employee retention rates, Wardour, 16 November 2023. www.wardour.co.uk/our-insights/why-everyones-focusing-on-employee-retention-rates.

[3] Management matters in an era of disruption: World Management Survey report 2024. https://poid.lse.ac.uk/textonly/publications/downloads/Management-matters-wms-2024.pdf.

[4] Management and UK 2030, the Chartered Management Institute. www.managers.org.uk/wp-content/uploads/2024/02/Management-and-UK-2030-Report-2024.pdf.

[5] State of the global workplace report 2023, Gallup. www.gallup.com/workplace/349484/state-of-the-global-workplace-2022-report.aspx.

[6] Top 5 Priorities for HR Leaders in 2025, Gartner. www.gartner.com/en/human-resources/trends/top-priorities-for-hr-leaders.

[7] Most managers believe flexible working helps productivity, UK study shows; a survey of 597 managers across the UK by the Equal Parenting Project, jointly resourced by the University of Birmingham and the University of York, 9 January 2023. www.theguardian.com/money/2023/jan/09/most-managers-believe-flexible-working-helps-productivity-uk-study-shows.

[8] Management matters in an era of disruption: World Management Survey report 2024. https://poid.lse.ac.uk/textonly/publications/downloads/Management-matters-wms-2024.pdf.

[9] State of the global workforce 2024, Gallup, October 2022. www.gallup.com/workplace/349484/state-of-the-global-workplace.aspx.

[10] Walking the walk, Chartered Management Institute, 2024. www.managers.org.uk/knowledge-and-insights/research/walking-the-walk/.

[11] Management and UK 2030, Chartered Management Institute, February 2024. www.managers.org.uk/wp-content/uploads/2024/02/Management-and-UK-2030-Report-2024.pdf.

[12] Over two-thirds of UK workers have quit or considered quitting their office job due to poor management, HR News, September 2024. https://hrnews.co.uk/over-two-thirds-of-uk-workers-have-quit-or-considered-quitting-their-office-job-due-to-poor-management/.

[13] Taking responsibility – why UK plc needs better managers, CMI and YouGov, October 2023. www.managers.org.uk/knowledge-and-insights/research/better-management-report-take-responsibility-take-action/.

[14] State of the global workforce 2024, Gallup, October 2022. www.gallup.com/workplace/349484/state-of-the-global-workplace.aspx.

[15] Management matters in an era of disruption: World Management Survey report 2024. https://poid.lse.ac.uk/textonly/publications/downloads/Management-matters-wms-2024.pdf.

Index

A quick word from Practical Inspiration Publishing...

We hope you found this book both practical and inspiring – that's what we aim for with every book we publish.

We publish titles on topics ranging from leadership, entrepreneurship, HR and marketing to self-development and wellbeing.

Find details of all our books at: www.practicalinspiration.com

Did you know...

We can offer discounts on bulk sales of all our titles – ideal if you want to use them for training purposes, corporate giveaways or simply because you feel these ideas deserve to be shared with your network.

We can even produce bespoke versions of our books, for example with your organization's logo and/or a tailored foreword.

To discuss further, contact us on info@practicalinspiration.com.

Got an idea for a business book?

We may be able to help. Find out about more about publishing in partnership with us at: bit.ly/PIpublishing.

Follow us on social media...

@PIPTalking

@pip_talking

@practicalinspiration

@piptalking

Practical Inspiration Publishing